WAITING FOR THE MOUNTAIN TO MOVE

WAITING FOR THE MOUNTAIN TO MOVE

❧ REFLECTIONS ON WORK AND LIFE

Charles Handy

Jossey-Bass Publishers
San Francisco

Jossey-Bass books and products are available through most bookstores. To contact Jossey-Bass directly, call (888) 378-2537, fax to (800) 605-2665, or visit our website at www.josseybass.com.

Substantial discounts on bulk quantities of Jossey-Bass books are available to corporations, professional associations, and other organizations. For details and discount information, contact the special sales department at Jossey-Bass.

 Manufactured in the United States of America on Lyons Falls Turin Book. This paper is acid-free and 100 percent totally chlorine-free.

Library of Congress Cataloging-in-Publication Data

Handy, Charles B.
    Waiting for the mountain to move : and other reflections on life / Charles Handy.
        p.   cm.
    Originally published: London : Arrow, 1992.
    ISBN 0-7879-4659-1 (alk. paper)
    1. Meditations.   2. Christian life.   I. Title.
BV4832.2.H277   1999
242—dc21   98-47908

HB Printing   10 9 8 7 6 5 4 3 2 1

CONTENTS

Waiting for the Mountain to Move

THE AUTHOR

℘ Charles Handy was born in Kildare, Ireland, in 1932, the
son of an archdeacon, and was educated in England
and the United States. He graduated from Oriel College, Oxford,
with first-class honors in Greats, the study of classics, history,
and philosophy. Handy has said that this discipline "gave me
the ability to think."

After college, Handy first worked for Shell International in
southeast Asia and London as a marketing executive, an econ-
omist, and a management educator. He then entered the Sloan
School of Management at the Massachusetts Institute of Technology. While there he became fascinated with organizations
and how they work. After he received his master's in business
administration from Sloan in 1967, he returned to England to
design and manage the only Sloan program outside the United
States, at Britain's first graduate business school, in London.

In 1972 Handy became a full professor of management
development at the school, specializing in managerial psychol-
ogy. From 1977 to 1981, he served as warden of St. George's
House in Windsor Castle, a private conference and study center concerned with ethics and values in society. He was chair of
the Royal Society of Arts in London from 1987 to 1989 and
holds honorary doctorates from four British universities. He is

known to many in Britain for his "Thoughts for the Day" on the BBC's radio program *Today*.

Handy's main concern has been the implications for society, and for individuals, of the dramatic changes that technology and economics are bringing to the workplace and to all our lives. His bestselling *The Age of Unreason* first explored these changes and was named by both *Fortune* and *Business Week* as one of the ten best business books of the year. The sequel, *The Age of Paradox*, was awarded the JSK Accord Prize for the best business book of 1994. In total, his books, which include *Gods of Management*, the standard textbook *Understanding Organizations*, *Understanding Schools as Organizations*, *Understanding Voluntary Organizations*, and *Inside Organizations*, have sold over a million copies around the world. An article for the *Harvard Business Review*, "Balancing Corporate Power: A New Federalist Paper," won the McKinsey Award for 1992, and another article for the same journal, "Trust and Virtual Organization," won the McKinsey Award in 1995. *Beyond Certainty* is a collection of his articles and essays. In his latest book, *The Hungry Spirit*, he surfaces some of his doubts about the consequences of free-market capitalism and questions whether material success can ever provide the true meaning of life.

Today, Handy is an independent author, teacher, and broadcaster focusing on the changing shape of work, organizations, and capitalism, which has an impact on every aspect of our lives. He describes himself now as a social philosopher. Handy and his wife, Elizabeth, a portrait photographer as well as his business partner, have two grown children and live in London and Norfolk, England, and in Tuscany. They have what Handy has termed "a portfolio life," balancing their skills and their time to make the most of their independent careers.

BY WAY OF
INTRODUCTION . . .

✍ "Would you like to do a 'Thought'?" asked Robert Foxcroft one day. I knew what he meant and, because I knew, was both flattered and surprised. "Thought" was short for "Thought for the Day," a three-minute religious reflection slotted between the news headlines and the weather every morning on the BBC's early-morning radio program *Today.* Robert was the producer. That question of Robert's, years later, gave birth to this book of reflections, or thoughts.

The god slot, as "Thought for the Day" was popularly known, was conventionally filled by bishops, priests, and rabbis, and I was none of those. But I was known to Robert, who acted as producer of this one daily spot as well as being vicar of St. Peter's Church in Hammersmith, London. Robert felt that I, as a rather renegade professor of business with theological affinities, might relate particularly to the many thousands of business and professional people who regularly tuned into this program.

"Actually," said Robert, "a few million people are listening, but don't get conceited; they won't have tuned in to listen to you. Half of them are in their cars and use the program to distract them from the thought of the day ahead; the others are naked in their bath or using the radio for wallpaper sound or an alarm clock as they go about their early morning chores.

Your task is to say something interesting so that they really start to listen."

I was, as I said, flattered. The first "Thought" was scheduled for months ahead. I had a holiday in Provence looming up, and I planned to use it to polish my ideas. I came back with some sample scripts. Robert read them carefully. "Yes," he said, "they're about right for length, but, well, this is supposed to be a thought for *the* day, not the encapsulated wisdom of a lifetime. Ideally, it needs to relate to something that's happening in the news or in your own life, a little nugget to chew on as they go to work." I tore them up and started again—or rather I learned not to start on them until the day before so that they would be fresh and relevant.

Sadly, Robert died not long afterward, to leave a huge gap in the lives of his many friends. I shall forever be grateful to him because he made me think—think about what mattered to me in life, think about my beliefs, such as they were, and how they came about, think particularly about how those beliefs shed light on the countless dilemmas and worries that seemed to make up the workaday world of myself and people like me.

Three minutes, 540 words or so. It doesn't sound like much, but it's the most difficult thing I ever had to do and in many ways the most rewarding—when and if it came out right. It is a great privilege to be allowed to share your personal beliefs with millions of others, whether they're listening or not, to be given three minutes with no interruptions, no questions asked, no editing. The presenters in the studio have no warning or knowledge of what I'm going to say, and the rules are that they must let me say it. I sometimes wonder what would happen if I abandoned my script and started to hurl abuse at the BBC, the prime minister, or the queen, calling down on them the wrath of God. Would anyone then interrupt?

Most of these reflections are slightly edited versions of those early-morning "Thoughts." Some arose from other occasions.

Waiting for the Mountain to Move

They spread over ten years, years that saw the end of the Cold War and the start of a Gulf War, as well as the goings and comings of prime ministers and presidents everywhere. Ten years that, nearer home and the lives of most of us, saw stock markets and housing markets boom and burst, earthquakes in San Francisco, and hurricanes in unusual places like southern England; but ten years, too, that saw the ups and downs of life in home and office continue as they always have, whatever happens in the big world outside.

My task, as I saw it, was to look for the meaning or the moral in those happenings, if there was one, and to put them all to the test of my beliefs. Sometimes I have thought that everyone ought to be invited to compose their own "thought for the day" because of the way it forces one to think. These reflections, therefore, are just that, my reflections on life as I see it happening around me. They carry no authority, they may well be heretical, they do not pretend to tell anyone else how to think; but if they goad or encourage people to do their own thinking about these things, I shall be well content.

The reflections reflect me. Inevitably. I have therefore added a "personal preface," in which I try to reveal a little more of me and the way my beliefs about life and the meaning of life came to be shaped.

ACKNOWLEDGMENTS

Every writer needs a friendly critic, every broadcaster a skilled producer, and every author an insightful publisher. I am lucky enough to have had all three to help bring these reflections to life.

Elizabeth, my wife, is the friendly critic. She keeps me honest and humble. "Speak from your heart," she tells me, "not from your head." And she is right because these are meant to be reflections, not sermons.

These reflections made their first appearance as "Thoughts for the Day" on the BBC's morning program. There, Robert Foxcroft was my first producer. I am grateful to him and to all his successors, most recently David Coomes, Christine Morgan, and Amanda Hancox. They coach me over the telephone lines, proving that you can have a wonderfully productive relationship with someone you never meet.

My British publishers, Gail Rebuck and Paul Sidey, made this book possible in the first place. Cedric Crocker at Jossey-Bass helped me share these thoughts with readers in the United States. I am endlessly grateful to them all for their creativity and support.

A PERSONAL PREFACE

It started, I suppose, with the death of my father. So many things do start with a death. It makes one wonder whom and what one's own death will spring loose.

My father was a quiet man. He had been rector of the same country parish in Kildare in southern Ireland for forty years when he retired, aged seventy-two. He was tired by then, understandably. For the last fourteen of those years he had also been archdeacon of the diocese. He died two years later.

I was in Paris at a business conference when I heard that he was dying. I flew back to Ireland, but he was unconscious by the time I got there and died the next day. His funeral, like all funerals in Ireland, was arranged for the day after tomorrow, a quiet family affair, back in the country church he had served for so long.

I was very fond of my father, but disappointed in him. He had turned down big-city parishes, had settled for a humdrum life in the same little backwater. His life seemed to be a series of boring meetings and visits punctuated with the unchanging rhythm of Sundays, with old Mrs. Atkinson and Eddie to lunch in the rectory afterward. As a teenager I resolved never to go to church again once I led my own life, and never to be poor again.

And so it was that, much to the amazement of my friends and family, I became an oil executive and was posted to the Far

East to be in charge of marketing in Sarawak—a job and a country both unknown in the rectory. I had a good time in Malaysia, mostly spending money and drinking too much beer. I came back fat and rather sleek, and also engaged to a beautiful English girl whom I had met in Kuala Lumpur.

She didn't think much of an oil executive's life or of her predestined role as an oil executive's hostess, so I switched to the newly discovered academic world of business studies, going to the United States to pick up another degree and coming back to the infant London Business School. Soon I was a professor, gallivanting around to conferences, consulting, lunching, dining, on the edge of the big time. A book had been published and articles galore. We had two young children, a flat in town, and a cottage in the country. More than that, I was tremendously busy, with a diary crammed with engagements. Success!

With these thoughts in mind I followed the hearse down the country roads to my father's funeral; a quiet end for a quiet man, I reflected. A pity that he never really understood what I was doing. When I became a professor, my mother's reaction to the news was to ask whether it meant that I could now spend more time with the children.

Suddenly I noticed that we seemed to have a police escort; the local police had decided unasked to clear our route for the last few miles to the church. A nice compliment to a Protestant vicar in rural Catholic Ireland, but just as well because it was hard to thread our way between the queues of cars trying to get to the little country church. The place was packed, overflowing. How had they heard? He had only died the day before yesterday, and there had been just the one notice in the paper.

The choir looked odd too. Dressed in the little-boy surplices that I remembered from Sundays long ago but with older faces. I remembered some of them. Choir boys and choir girls reassembled from all the corners of Ireland, and from England too. They had dropped everything to be there. The archbishop, supposed to be in the hospital and still propped on a stick, was there to say to all of us how special my father had been and how he would be missed but remembered forever by so many whose lives he had touched.

As I stood by his grave, surrounded by people he had helped to marry and whose children he had later baptized and then seen marry in his church in their turn, as I saw the tears in the eyes of the hundreds of people who had come from everywhere to say farewell to this "quiet" man, I turned away and began to think.

Who, I wondered, would come to my funeral with tears in their eyes? What is success and who was successful, me or my father? What is one's life for, and what is the point of our existence in this world? They are not exactly new questions. I had studied philosophy. I knew the theories. I had never applied them to myself before. Not seriously.

I went back to England. It was a long, hot summer that year. I resolved to change my life and my priorities. I thought I might go to theological college, might become ordained, be a priest like my father. Luckily, I now think, the bishops whom I approached told me not to be so silly. If I wanted to serve God, as they put it, I could do it much better as a professor of business than in a dog collar.

They encouraged me to apply for the post of warden of St. George's House in Windsor Castle. This small, select study center was established by Prince Philip and the then dean of Windsor, Robin Woods, to be a meeting place for people of influence in the churches and in other parts of society. It ran consultations on topics like justice, the future of work, power, and responsibility in our institutions—consultations at which captains of industry, trade-union leaders, head teachers, civil servants, and politicians mingled and debated with bishops and chaplains and each other. It was a place of retreat and reflection for busy people in a busy world, set in a courtyard behind St. George's Chapel. It became my home and my obsession for the next four years.

From one extreme to another. I thought at first that they had left out a nought when I saw my salary. They provided me with a lovely house, but the cost of carpeting it was more than my first year's pay. What was all this about never being poor again, I wondered. Life has a way of going full circle, and as for never going to church again, I lived in the shadow of the great Chapel of St. George and attended with relish the early-morning service there in the little upstairs chapel every day of every week. "You've been to church three times this week," my startled mother-in-law said to my wife and myself once, "and it's only Thursday!"

But I was also in charge of the study center and was experiencing all the problems of moving into a new institution in a new field, a world where I was not known and where I knew not its ways. It was stressful. Before long I took myself off to a psychotherapist. "What are you seeking to achieve?" he asked me. "I just want to make the world, in some small way, a better place," I replied. "Oh, I see," he said with heavy irony, "so now we have the three of you, Jesus Christ, the Prophet Mohammed, and Professor Charles Handy!" I blushed, rebuked and embarrassed, but I got the message: here I was sitting in his consulting room, sick at heart, and talking about changing the world. There was something somewhere about taking great beams out of one's own eyes first, I recalled. I needed to be surer about myself and my beliefs if I was going to be of any use to anyone else. To put it more crisply, being is essential to doing; who I am colors what I do. Was it not Dr. Johnson who said, "Who you are sounds so loudly in my ears that I can't hear what you say"?

He said something else, my psychotherapist. I had arrived late for one session. Hampstead is a long way from Windsor and the traffic can be bad. I got there at twenty minutes past the hour instead of on the hour. At 2:50 P.M. when I had been there thirty minutes his little alarm went "ping," signaling that the normal fifty-minute consultation was up. "Oh dear," I said, "I've only just got going. Have you anyone else coming?"

"No," he said.

"Well, then, can I stay on?"

"No, I'm afraid not."

"But I've only been here thirty minutes. I got delayed by the traffic."

"That's your problem," he said, "not mine."

I went away fuming, but then I reflected that he was right. I spent my life apologizing to people for things that had nothing to do with me, like the weather, the state of our street, or the rudeness of the local shopkeeper. If people arrived late, *I* didn't cut short the appointment; I said, "Oh bad luck, please don't concern yourself," and would cheerfully change my plans for the day because of *their* poor scheduling, taking, as it were, their failings on my shoulders and feeling noble as I did it. This was, I now saw, to take responsibility away from them, to steal their choices. But was not this what Jesus Christ was supposed to have done, taken all our sins on himself? No, I eventually decided, that had to be a misrepresentation of Christianity. It is not an escapist religion. We can't go off and do as we like and then dump all our sins or mistakes on the deity. That's garbage-can religion with God as the garbage can.

I was beginning to realize not only that theology was not as straightforward as it had seemed in the days of my youth but that it was also highly practical. I could not get on with my life or be at peace with myself until I had sorted out some of this stuff. Being and doing are inseparable.

Two months later I was invited by the dean and canons to preach the sermon at the Sunday morning service in St. George's Chapel. It was, I was told, the first time a layman had preached formally in that place since it was built in the sixteenth century. I was suitably overawed. I decided that it would be quite inappropriate for me to try to interpret the word of God so instead I set out to explain what I saw as the point and purpose of the study center that sat at the end of the courtyard at the back of the chapel. It was, I said, a place where we tried to connect people's beliefs with the problems of life and of work in today's world. If I am right, I said, the central message of Christianity is that religion is not about another life in another world but about our life in this world—God became Man, as the Bible puts it. The search for that connection between belief and action is never-ending and always changing because the world and its problems are always changing. The beliefs may remain the same, but their applications will always need to be rethought by each of us each year, even each day. We are forever going to be searchers after truth.

I need not have worried too much about my sermon. I had forgotten about the verger. The verger, who is the master of ceremonies on these occasions, had never been too keen on the idea. "Sit where you like," he had said when I asked him about the protocol, "and wear what you like. This has never happened before. There is no precedent." I got the distinct impression that he hoped it would never happen again. I should not therefore have been terribly surprised when the microphones failed just after I got up to speak and did not function again that morning. The ears of the faithful were not afflicted by any possible heresies that day, and I learned, yet again, that those who control the technology always wield great negative power, so it is as well to have them on your side. I was pleased when the verger came up to me the next day to apologize for a "malfunctioning of the audio system" and also to ask for a copy of my address. "Those who heard it said that it made a lot of sense." But that, of course, was afterward.

The ears of the faithful may not have been harmed, but I learned a lot. It was an Irishman who said, "How do I know what I think until I hear what I say?" and I am an Irishman. It remains the best clue to learning that I know of. The need to communicate forces you to work out what you want to say, and, after that, it doesn't matter too much if anyone listens or not because what they ought to do is to work out in their turn what they want to say. Preaching, you might say, gets in the way of learning, except for the preacher.

Over four years I listened to some six thousand people in small seminars and consultations find out what they thought when they heard what they said. Some of what they said was inspiring, some was boring, some bizarre. You couldn't always predict which mouths would say which. Two years after I left the place a businessman asked me to lunch, to thank me he said. "What for?" I asked, over the drinks. "Because of that weekend in Windsor some years back. I heard myself saying that the sense of responsibility that goes with ownership is so important that it shouldn't be a minority right. I went away and thought about that and decided to share the ownership of my business with my workers. The agreement was signed yesterday, hence this lunch."

Has this anything to do with religion—I used to ask myself—with the hymns and the psalms the choir sings so beautifully in that chapel? I'm sure it does. I'm sure that our beliefs should, and do, infect our lives. If we try to live our lives in separate compartments, one for doing, perhaps, and one for being, then for part of the time we are living a lie, "the truth is not in us." That I found and still find is not very comfortable.

Since the day of that sermon I have been trying to bring my being and my doing closer together. In time I left Windsor. It was time to go anyway, but I was growing increasingly uncomfortable with the need to fit into my role. It is hard for being and doing to weld into one when for part of your doing you have to act a part that is not totally "you." All of us, in organizations, are "role occupants," and few of us could claim that there is a perfect match between us and our role. That, I think, is part of the problem with organizations and part of their seduction. They force us, or allow us, depending on your viewpoint, to escape from ourselves and to play a part. It can be fun for a while. It can be damaging in the end.

To me the only answer, I gradually realized, was to be my own master and employer. Today I am a self-employed writer and teacher. It is financially more perilous but in every other way more secure. I can't now escape from myself in my work, but these days I don't want to so much. Being and doing are closer.

It is no part of my mission to foist my beliefs onto other people. That would run counter to my philosophy of life and learning. We each have to do the searching for ourselves. Nevertheless, some clues to my beliefs can be found in these reflections. My concern is only to point to what *I* see as the meaning in things and to the ultimate purpose in life in order to encourage other people to find their meaning and their purpose. The nicest comments I ever had on those broadcasts were from the man who said, "You set me thinking for the whole of that day," and from the woman who wrote, "I had been bedridden for three years bemoaning my bad luck in losing both my legs. After listening, I decided that I had to do something with my life so I got up and enrolled in the local college."

WAITING FOR THE MOUNTAIN TO MOVE

WAITING FOR THE MOUNTAIN TO MOVE

When I get depressed, I try to think of the unemployed British laborer who, famously, thrust his thousand job-rejection letters under the prime minister's nose on her tour of his region and stole all her glory from her for a day. Two weeks later he got a placement with a job-training scheme, learning to be a printer, armed, moreover, with an interview report which describes him as bright, capable, and articulate.

Mind you, I always thought that he was underselling himself when he described himself as "just a laboring man," incapable of learning a new skill. Anyone who has the stamina to apply for a thousand jobs and the gumption to present them to a prime minister has to have *something* going for him.

I hope it works out for him because it might mean a change not just in his living standards but in the whole way he looks at life. It was, I think, the sense of helplessness which he projected and which had, apparently, infected his whole family that made so many identify with him but exasperated so many others.

But I have, myself, had a glimpse of how he must have felt. My blackest times are those when I feel that my life is out of my control. Things are happening, or not happening, and I seem powerless to stop them or change them. It then gets even

1

worse when I start to hope, yes and sometimes pray, that some outside being will intervene to put things right and *still* nothing happens.

It reminds me of Kierkegaard's story of the traveler in the hill country who came to a village only to find his road onward blocked by a mountain. So he sat and waited for the mountain to move. Years later he was still there, old now and white-haired, still waiting. Then he died, but he was long remembered in the village as a proverb, "the man who waited for the mountain to move."

Kierkegaard's point is that God doesn't move mountains (or send stock markets crashing); *we climb* mountains with God's help. Don't therefore look for Him, or His agent, outside. Look for Him inside, in *you*, and using His eyes find *new* bits of you which you never knew were there.

I go along with the fourteenth-century author of that great mystical work *The Cloud of Unknowing*. "Swink and sweat in all that thou canst and mayest," he says, "for to get thee a true knowing and feeling of thyself as thou art. And then, I trow, soon after that thou wilt get thee a true knowing and feeling of God as He is." There is, you see, more to all of us than we think there is. We *must* believe that. Swink and sweat to find yourself. It has to be worth it.

BUFFALO BILL
OR ME?

℘ What's in a name? Quite a lot, seemingly. At any rate lots of us are at it—changing names, that is. Companies do it, sometimes with bewildering rapidity; designing company logos is the new growth industry. Whole countries do it. People do it, particularly when they marry or unmarry. I dropped the name Charlie when I went to college and became Charles—a sign of my accelerating pomposity, my parents said then.

Changing one's name is, it seems, a self-awarded license to be different. In fact, many people these days do *not* change their names when they marry—a signal perhaps that they do *not* intend to be different. And I remember long ago going to a rather trendy workshop in the United States where you were invited to invent a new name before you came with a promise that no one, not even the seminar leader, would know your real one. There were two Buffalo Bills, I recall, in that group, one Marilyn Monroe and one Anon. After much agony I went as myself, ashamed at first of my lack of imagination, then proud of my integrity. What it meant, however, the seminar leader told me, was that I was there under false pretenses—I didn't want to find a new "me."

A new name, however, is only the start of it. The name signals a determination to be different, to have a new beginning,

3

a rebirth even, but who then will we decide to be? Oneself, I hope. I used to tell my students not to look over their shoulders, meaning that they did not need to ape their colleagues, that they should set their *own* standards and make their *own* definitions of success.

Bishop Richard Harries, in one of his books, has a nice story about a rabbi with an unpronounceable name, Zuzya of Hannipol. "'In the coming world,' said the rabbi, 'they will not ask me why was I not Moses but why was I not Zuzya.'" And, as for me, I don't want to die knowing that I had only pretended to live.

So how do I know when I'm me? It's a good question for all of us—individuals, companies, political parties even. It's like beauty, I think, or being in tune. You can't define it, but you know when it's there and when it's not there. You have to trust your eye or your ear, and you have, above all, to believe that there is a tune for you, or as St. Paul put it to the cosmopolitan and fun-loving Corinthians, the yuppies of yesteryear, you must believe that the Spirit is in each and every one of us, with a different message for each but for the good of all. If you don't believe that you'll just be a sounding brass or a clashing cymbal, or today a portable fax and a personal phone.

POPE LEO X
AND KANT

☙ It's a nice coincidence that the Americans are going to the polls on Guy Fawkes day. This is the day when we are supposed to be celebrating the fact that Parliament survived Mr. Fawkes and his plot to blow it up, that democracy was saved for the nation. You would think, from the way we traditionally celebrate the event, that most of us wish he had succeeded, but then, as Churchill observed, democracy is the worst form of government—except for all the alternatives.

But if democracy is so important, despite its flaws, why are so many Americans going to stay at home today, as everyone is forecasting? "A plague on both their houses" they seem to be saying, or "They're all the same—it makes no difference." Maybe they are right. Tom Paine, another man from Norfolk, where I'm speaking now, said that government at its best was a necessary nuisance, but at its worst it was a disaster. So, people say, as long as it's not a disaster, let's just get on with our lives. Maybe they realize that democracy means much more than casting a vote every four years or so. Democracy means that the people have the control not just over who should govern them but over their own lives, and that is what really matters.

If you want to be technical, it is called the principle of subsidiarity. I wish that the word wasn't so ugly because it is so crucial. It means that stealing other people's decisions is morally wrong. Pope Leo X said so, back in the Renaissance, so subsidiarity isn't some modern invention to keep Brussels at bay, it reaches into every crevice of our lives. Take marriage. You won't believe this, but when I first started to work, my company, an international oil company, insisted on approving my choice of a wife. They didn't trust me to get it right! Correctly so, actually, because when I did get married the first thing my wife did was to get me to resign. Even today, my Indian friends think that we are crazy to let our grown-up kids choose their partners. Young people are so impetuous, they say. Yes, I reply but it is *their* life.

So I tell them about Pope Leo, a bad man but a good pope (maybe the two can go together, Americans please note), and the moral principle that we should each have as much responsibility for our lives as we can bear. I also stress that we have to educate people to carry that responsibility. I tell them, therefore, about Immanuel Kant, another important man that more young people should know about, whose principle of morality was that whatever was right for you must also be OK for everyone else. Think about that long enough, and you end up with quite a free but decent society, a good democracy.

ON PLANTING
A WALNUT TREE

&⁊ Earlier this year I planted a walnut tree. It's a strange feeling, planting walnut trees. You know that you are never going to see that tree looking as a walnut tree should, old and gnarled and venerable and full of nuts. Some day, perhaps, your grandchildren, or more likely some stranger's grandchildren, will look up and say, "Doesn't that walnut look great," or will curse it when the nuts get in the way of the lawnmower. They won't thank you or curse you; they won't even think of there being a you, someone who once consciously decided to plant that tree in that place. So why was I doing it? I won't see it grown up; no one will thank me for it or remember me for it. I guess I planted it because it just seemed right and would seem right in the days after I was gone. It was, I must admit, a good feeling. I wondered why such an irrational act felt so good. It set me thinking.

I wondered first why so little of the rest of my life had this kind of perspective. I was, most of the time, more like a sower of annual flowers, looking for results this summer, or at best a planter of shrubs which have a three-year payoff. Yet I remembered the head of a family business telling me that the great family businesses were great partly because the family members found it natural to "think beyond the grave." Their successors would be their children and their children's children. It was easier therefore to make decisions which would not pay off in their time but only in the next generation. This gave them, he said, the sense of perspective, and of long-term strategy, which so many businesses find it so hard to cultivate.

I remembered, too, a discussion about the dilemmas of modern politicians, who live with the constant need to win the next election, which is on average only two-and-a-bit years away, yet have, on taking office, to decide on policies which may not produce results for ten years or more. "Who," asked someone, "is looking after our grandchildren when those who govern us are looking after the next election? Is it right, for instance, to build up a huge financial deficit today in order to create more jobs, which is effectively borrowing from the grandchildren to keep the grandparents comfortable?"

"Thinking beyond the grave." It's a nice phrase. Living now so that others later can live more abundantly. Life after death, but *others'* lives after *your* death. Perhaps that is part of what Christianity is really all about.

STICKING POINTS

I'm lucky, I suppose. I've never really been pushed up against death. I don't know how I would behave in a hijack; I'm rather afraid that the answer might be "shamefully." Lucky? Well, on second thought, perhaps not so lucky because I've never had to work out what my sticking points are.

Sticking points. The bishop used the word when he was with me and a group of managers some years back. "What's your sticking point?" he asked them. "What would you not do, no matter what?" "Murder," they said, "or steal or lie." Yet, on reflection, they weren't so sure. Would you not lie to save your life on that hijacked plane if you thought it would work? Would you lie, or at least conceal the truth, to do a better deal in business? To sell your house or trade in your car?

The bishop's point, I think, was that all life is based on some assumption of principle. There can never be enough laws and rules and inspectors to cover everything, particularly in organizations and in business, even in families. Life would get too complicated—and too expensive.

I remember taking a group of clergy some years back to see around the Lloyd's insurance building and to meet some of the agents, underwriters, and brokers, and, finally, the chairman himself. "Very impressive it is," said the clergy; "it all seems very efficient, but it must be tremendously testing morally."

The chairman looked bemused, I remember. "Why?" he asked. "Well," they said, "everyone seems to have two or more roles, two or more conflicting loyalties; there aren't many rules or inspectors, so you have to trust people to act on principle, honorably." "Of course," he said. Alas, not long after, Lloyd's had the famous failure, proving that unprincipled people can thrive in a system based mainly on principle.

It was ironic, I reflected then, that just as Lloyd's had begun to make more rules and to put up some barriers between its conflicting loyalties, the stock market started to dismantle its barriers in order to remain competitive. Nobody realized at the time that the so-called big bang was going to make principle and people of principle even more precious in London's financial world—the City.

And not just in the City. If organizations of any sort are to be left reasonably unfettered, if individuals are to be free to exercise their own initiative, then one's personal principles and values cannot be left on the coatrack when you walk through the office door. Principles don't belong in one box, work in another, even if it would be convenient for some of us to think that they do.

Indeed, I do know some people who seem to operate with two sets of principles—one Sunday-best for home consumption, another more, shall we say, pragmatic for downtown. They call it sensible. I call it moral schizophrenia and a recipe for breakdown both of the individual and the organization.

I don't think it's an accident that, on the whole, the most efficient organizations are the most principled ones. Trust, after all, costs much less than checking; but for trust to work you need to have principles and sticking points, and they come only, I believe, from a set of beliefs.

IDIOSYNCRACY CREDITS

᳃ Last night I laughed at the opera. I think it was permissible because it was Benjamin Britten's funny opera—*Albert Herring*—even though it ends up as a potential tragedy. It's about a young village lad, the model of good behavior, who breaks loose one day, has a night on the town, and comes back dirty and disheveled but a new man, having discovered bits of his real self. But he has also disgraced his mother and outraged the neighbors, and you sense, at the end, that he has no future in that village or anywhere else.

What price freedom and individuality, I wondered as I left, if it results in social ostracism? On the other hand, who would want to live their life by other people's rules? It seems, sometimes, that you can't win. I grew up in a time when you were expected to behave the way your elders behaved, and I felt boxed in and frustrated. My children grew up in an age of much greater freedom, but I suspect that they feel equally confused at times, having to invent all their own codes of behavior and definitions of success. Which is more important—individuality or respect for the rules?

Well, we are all unique; I'm convinced of that. Why else would we each have our own thumbprint and eyeball, soon to be encoded on our personal smart cards? Given that fact, I believe that it is morally incumbent on us to live up to that

11

uniqueness, to discover and be ourselves. Yet that sort of individualist philosophy, if carried to extremes, leads to a very self-centered world, one where anything goes if it works for you and it's legal. It's a world without too many accepted moral principles, and because those aren't around, we have to have more laws and rules to hold the place together. If I'm not interested in my neighbor, then we shall have to pass a law to make sure that I'm not a nuisance to him. An individualized world is one made for lawyers. And who, apart from lawyers, wants that?

So we need both, individualism mixed with some proper respect for the norms of your bit of society. But how do you balance the two? I remembered, then, an old idea from the study of organizations. It's the notion of idiosyncracy credits, a notion which says that you have to earn the right to be different. Only when people recognize that you are making a contribution can you safely stretch things a bit. The bore is, as I discovered once, to my dismay, that you can't run an idiosyncracy overdraft. You can't be different first and earn the right later. Put another way, only if you *first* show proper consideration for others are you free to be fully yourself. It isn't only me, I have to remind myself, who is unique.

NEGATIVE CAPABILITY

ɮ Uncertainty, they say, is part of the human condition. I sometimes wonder, however, just how much uncertainty our human condition can stand.

I don't remember a time when the news has been so compelling, everywhere. Change is in the air, like spring—heady, and frightening. The neatest bit of news that I saw, in December 1989, when walls were falling all over Europe, was an item in the *International Herald Tribune*. "5000 Alsatian guard-dogs surplus in East Germany," the headline said. "Too violent to be used as household pets." It was, I felt, an apt symbol of the end of the Cold War. But then I spared a thought or two for the person who had had what he or she thought was a secure business breeding and training Alsatian dogs to prowl the wall. A nice little niche market, you might say, destroyed overnight. Change is *not* heady when it happens to you—just frightening.

Most of us therefore hope and pray that it won't happen to us. "Why cannot the status quo be the way forward?" someone once wistfully asked. The Old Testament psalmist was more realistic. "It is the fool and the brutish person," he wrote, "who in their inward thoughts think that their houses will continue forever, their dwelling places for all generations, who call their lands after their own names." We should be so lucky.

Product life cycles are down to six months in some businesses. Models are out of date before you've read the ads. What was a meadow in January is a motorway in November. You had best assume that next year is an unsolved problem for which last year's solutions provide no help. Uncertainty, as I have said, is part of the human condition.

Another poet, Keats this time, had an answer. Negative capability, that's what's needed he said; negative capability, which he defined as when a man is capable of being in *uncertainties, mysteries,* and *doubts.* Negative capability—the strength to keep going when all about you is in flux, when the future is a blank sheet of paper waiting for you to write on it. Let us hope that President Clinton has his cup flowing over with it.

Negative capability—it's an ugly phrase for a poet to use. I prefer the pillar of cloud by day and pillar of fire by night that was God's sign of reassurance to the Israelites in the wilderness. That's what religion has always been about, not certainty, but the strength to live with *uncertainty,* in the wilderness, in the face of death. Negative capability—I guess it's a jargon word for *faith.*

TRUST AND
THE PLUMBER

ℬ Compared with all the dramas being acted out on the news these days my problems with my plumber may sound trivial. But they too may be clues to the world we live in, a barometer on the weather ahead. He's a nice chap, our plumber, and I trust him, so when I asked him to fit an outside tap on the garden wall and agreed to a price I thought that that was that.

He fixed the tap all right, but instead of putting it above the gully so that any drips would drain away he had put it three feet to the left, where it would slop all over the grass. I could see why; it was easier for him to put it there and he was always one for the shortcut. When I complained, he said, "Oh, it's against Water Board regulations to put a tap above a drain. Contamination you see." It sounded a bit odd, but, as I said, he's a nice chap and I trusted him.

"Don't be silly," said my wife, "he's having you on." She rang the Water Board and of course he *was* talking nonsense, telling lies to get himself out of a corner.

Well, I forgave him because I wanted him to sort it out; and he did, reluctantly. But I seem to have been required to forgive an awful lot of people lately for broken promises, missed deadlines, bad work, or lost money—people I trusted but who let me down.

15

Can it be, I wondered, as I sat, like Job, on the building site that should have been my home, that I am really expected to take books like the Bible seriously when it says that I should forgive my brother seventy times seven when he let me down every single time? The answer, I'm afraid, is "yes" if I want him to continue to be my brother. That's not piety, that's practicality, because no relationship can survive and grow unless we are prepared to trust and to forgive when the trust goes wrong, again and again and again. No forgiveness means no relationship.

That's the bad weather which I feel coming in our society today. Trust and forgiveness are not much in evidence today because too often neither party cares whether the relationship continues or not, neither supplier nor customer, neither organization nor contractor, sometimes neither husband nor wife. Enterprise can then come to mean "getting away with it"; prudent people will "trust but verify," as President Reagan used to say, while careful people watch their backs and call their lawyers.

It's a sad world, I think, when we can genuinely pray "forgive us for *not* forgiving those who sin against us." It's a sign that trust and love and friendship have failed, have become the luxuries of life but not its basics. For myself, I will try to choose my plumbers better and *then* will persevere, trusting against the odds, forgiving if I can because, in the end, relationships matter more than perfect plumbing, and trust is cheaper than lawyers.

LAST MONTH WE CLOSED A FACTORY

_L_ ast month we closed a factory. When I say "we," I mean the small business of which I am a part-time director.

I don't suppose that these decisions are ever taken lightly, and this one certainly wasn't. But we had to face the facts: the factory had been losing money for two years, and we could not let it bleed the rest of the business to death.

The business logic was clear. The human logic was just awful. How do you explain to people who have been working harder than ever and producing more than ever before that it was all useless; the stuff still sold at a loss, the more they made the more we lost. Economics can be a baffling science.

We listened to men, and women, telling us what it would be like to lose their jobs in an area where there were no new jobs. Many would never have a paid job again, and it wouldn't be their fault. I felt like a judge passing sentence on the innocent.

Whose fault _was_ it? Some said it was ours for not keeping them in jobs until all the money ran out, just in case things turned up. But we saw, all too clearly, that if we didn't close that factory now the whole lot would go. Isn't it better that some should go so that others might live? Not if it's you that goes, it isn't. It may be glorious to die for one's country, but it isn't yet glorious to be made redundant for your firm. Should it be?

Some knew it was no one's fault. Nothing lasts forever. New technology, or new habits, put paid to many things we took for granted. The candles I went to bed with every night when I was a boy in the depths of the country are now, for us, kept for special occasions. The electric light is easier for us, but it was tough on the candle makers. Death and then new life, in business as in nature. It's OK if it's nature and winter is followed by spring, but it's tougher in business, where only winter is on offer, and spring is in other parts of the country and for other skills.

"Get on your bike then," the man said, but did he know that only 10 percent of the unemployed have bikes?

Some blamed the system. "If it all belonged to everyone, then everyone could have jobs," they said. Not in that plant they couldn't, and not at those wages. You can change the owners, but that doesn't change the cost of the product.

Some accused us of playing God. We were, they thought, sitting in that peculiar kind of heaven called a board room disposing of people's lives to suit our own grand design. Playing God? It didn't feel like that at all, unfortunately, at least not my kind of god.

My god would have found a way to give *each individual* the glimpse of new life in this kind of death and the means to grasp that life. My god would have found some light to shine on each person's darkness, some way of giving new meaning to each life, some way of discovering new talents in each of them and pushing them toward new opportunities. My god would have made them feel sure that they lived on, even when the factory died.

We did our best to do all this, but I'm afraid it won't be enough for many at that plant, and many won't even believe we meant it. After all, institutions, no matter how well-intentioned, no matter who owns them or runs them, are no match for God. Perhaps no one should expect them to be.

CHINDOGU

ॐ The first snow has now fallen, but no one has yet told me how many shopping days there are to Christmas. They soon will because the chindogu festival is with us again! What is chindogu? you may well ask. Chindogu is a Japanese word for all the useless things we might be tempted to buy—windscreen wipers for your spectacles in case you go out in the rain, slippers with mops underneath so that you can polish the floor as you walk around the house. I have all those ties that I'm never going to use—chindogu. There is going to be a lot of it wrapped up in fancy papers in a few weeks time, and more chindogu catalogues come through my door with every post.

Chindogu can get exotic. A friend of mine visiting someone in Brazil found that he had six fridges in his house, five of them not plugged in. Why? he asked. Well, the Brazilian explained, when inflation was at its height here, money went off very quickly, like milk in the sun; so as soon as I had any, I went out and spent it, and the only things I fancied were fridges—so, chindogu fridges. Is this what "buoyant consumer demand" really means? Is this what we are all working so hard for? In a hundred years, if we maintain our growth rate of 3 percent, we shall be consuming sixteen times as much of everything. Well, we won't need sixteen times as many cars, or television sets, or washing machines, so a lot of it is going to be more chindogu, things or services we don't really need.

Getting and spending we lay waste our powers, said Wordsworth, and that was a century ago. It hasn't changed. I think that we might, today, usefully remember the old theological doctrine of enough, which holds that unless you define what enough means for you, in money and worldly goods, you are not free to do what you ought to be doing; you are endlessly wanting more, perpetually dissatisfied. The churches translated this into the stipendiary principle. My father was a parson. He had a stipend, a smart word for a salary, but the principle was different; a stipend was intended to be just enough to cover his material needs so that he could get on with his proper work. Money was not the measure of anything he did.

If one takes this "enough" business seriously, it turns out that the freest people, in time as well as possibilities, are those who set the level of enough rather low. Maybe that's why the poor in heart, those who choose to be poor, are called blessed. Of course it would play havoc with the GNP statistics if we all stopped buying chindogu and lowered our definitions of enough, but maybe it's time, anyway, that we revised our definitions of growth for society and of success for ourselves. Perhaps the arrival of our annual chindogu festival may be a good time for a reassessment.

TYPE TWO
ACCOUNTABILITY

It's Budget Day! I have always thought that it was pleasingly symbolic that Budget Day should fall in Lent, the period of abstinence—although, if you believe the hype, it may feel more like Christmas this time round. But what the government calls a Budget isn't quite like the budgets some of us know and love at work and at home. *Those* budgets are really all about targets and limits, and you get held accountable for meeting them a year later. Accountability. Now there's a thought. Maybe each Budget Day should start with an independent review of how the last Budget worked out.

Accountability, however, turns out to be quite a tricky notion when you get into it. I was taught once, in my business school, that there were two types of error: Type One errors, which mean getting it wrong, and Type Two errors, which mean not getting it right enough, missing the opportunities. It's an important difference. Most organizations that I know get besotted about Type One errors, the mistakes that are always easy to spot. They don't notice the Type Two errors, the chances to do things even better, even to do things no one thought of. Accountability's the same; it comes in two types. Type One is our responsibility for not getting it wrong; Type Two, for making it better than it otherwise would have been.

I sometimes think it's one of those British diseases, this tendency to focus on Type One errors. Even if it's not, it certainly pervades the British tradition of Christianity. Sin, in our churches, always seems to be Type One errors, the things I did wrong. Keep your nose clean and you'll be all right seems to be the message. Nearly all the commandments are *not* commandments, Type One commandments. I find it highly depressing.

But that's not the way it's meant to be. Jesus put the commandments more positively. Love God and love your neighbor, he said—if I may summarize—that's all you know on earth and all you need to know. Actually, that last bit is Keats, but I think that Jesus would have liked it! Now love, as I have eventually come to realize, is not just about doing right by someone, avoiding those Type One errors; it's about making things happen with or for someone which would never have happened otherwise, making the world wonderfully better for them. That's Type Two accountability. And that's a challenge I can get excited about.

Come to think of it, when I used to go to Matins or Morning Prayer in the days when such things were said in our churches, I remember asking for forgiveness "because we have left undone all those things we ought to have done, and have done those things we ought not to have done." There it is. Type Two errors and Type One errors, but rather more elegantly phrased than in my business school. But these days, as I get too old to break most of those Type One commandments, it's Type Two accountability which is key to my personal budget this Budget Day.

COMPROMISE

It is encouraging to hear the word *compromise* being mentioned so often by all concerned in the Northern Ireland talks this week. Long may it continue because in all arguments and disputes, indeed in all relationships, compromise is the only way forward. Compromise means that there are no winners, but then victories in relationships are usually Pyrrhic, in that the winner suffers more than the loser, or else are very short-lived. "All right, you win," my wife often says to me, "but I'm right." That's when I know that I have really lost!

The trouble is that compromise means that both sides have to forgive and forget the past. History has to be put to bed. No more references to "that time when you . . ."—whatever it was you did or said. Private dreams have to be dropped, too, and that may be harder still. In their place one needs a new dream, a shared dream, a dream in which there is something for all, something which will be better, if it comes to pass, than the old dreams which will never make it. We must hope that the dream of a peaceful land in the north of Ireland will be powerful enough to allow people to lay their old histories, dreams, and fears to rest.

Fear matters because for the new dream to work you have to trust each other. But—catch-22—you can't trust anyone until you have worked with them. To realize the dream there has to be, therefore, that great leap of faith, in each other and in the value of the dream. Religions at their best know that although, sadly, their practice does not always match their preaching. Great teams know that, and great leaders know that their main task is to make the shared dream so real and so important that it drowns out all previous history, all fears, and all petty rivalries. But it happens on a smaller and more personal plane too. I like to say that like many people of my age I am now on my second marriage, but it is to the same woman, which keeps it in the family you might say.

When we were younger, we were bonded together by a common dream of homemaking and children. But the homes got made and the children grew up. It was a time for private dreams and personal ambitions, which often got in each other's way. Compromise was needed if we were to stay together. Victory for one or the other would have meant defeat for both because we would have split. So we talked. With some difficulty we worked out a shared dream which gave us each a role in a common project—our life together. The dream needs constant reworking, but we know now that compromise is the best way forward for each of us because neither of us would be as good without the other. I wish the same for the people of Northern Ireland and for all who are at loggerheads this morning.

SEVEN
INTELLIGENCES

✑ I was vicariously proud when my young cousin Gillian went off to St. James's Palace to collect her gold award in the Duke of Edinburgh's Award Scheme. This scheme, with its emphasis on social and practical skills, on adventure and discovery, and on service to others reminds me that not all learning takes place in the classroom. Just as well, one might think, given the worries expressed by the chief inspector of England's schools when he warned that the whole education service might collapse without a lot more qualified and competent teachers.

That month, too, my two-and-a-half-year-old niece was threatened with expulsion from her playgroup for demanding one-to-one attention. She will go far, that girl; but she won't get her way in English schools, where soon there may not be enough teachers for one-to-fifty in some subjects.

We must heed these warnings. Surely, we must not ration learning, for God did not ration our human potential, He just calls it different names in different people. I revel in the research which has pinned down seven different types of intelligence. There's the intellectual intelligence, of course, but also the musical intelligence, the creative intelligence, the practical and the physical, the social and the psychic.

Yes, in that sense pop musicians are intelligent, so are footballers, so are those who can take a carburetor to bits and put it together again but could not spell it to save their lives. Call it talent if you prefer, but I like the thought that we are all intelligent in our own way.

What is interesting is that the intelligences are not connected, so that the girl who is a dunce in class can be a wow as a bond dealer, or the expert scaffold maker can be hopeless at the geometry he practices. "Oh, he's intellectual all right," complained my daughter of her scholarly friend, "but practical he's not; he couldn't run a bath let alone that band of his."

St. Paul was making the same kind of point when he told the worldly-wise Corinthians that the gifts of the Spirit came in different forms to different people, but all were as necessary as the different parts of the body are to health. Life would be awful if we were all the same. It's when I look around at my friends that I now realize how each of them is intelligent in his or her own way, although I never looked at it that way before.

To me, now, it is an article of faith that everyone is intelligent in some way. The challenge is to find the way. Some never do. They are our sadness. But for the future let us at least make sure that all our children discover that they are intelligent in their own particular way, in or out of school, before they get trapped into jobs or lives where they cannot shine. Then no one need feel stupid anymore.

HOME FOR
CHRISTMAS

꙳ "I've changed my mind. I wanted to have a telescope,
but now I want my daddy back." Lucien Lawrence's
letter to Father Christmas, written after his schoolteacher father
had been knifed to death outside his own school gate, must have
touched every heart. Lucien went on to say that without his
father there he can't see the stars in the sky. Literally and
metaphorically how true that can be. When those whom we love
depart from us, then we, too, can no longer see the stars for a
while.

But, Lucien, the stars are still there, and one day, when
you are older and the mist of tears has gone, you will see them
again, by yourself. And, in a strange way, I expect that you will
find that your father is there too, in your mind and in your
heart. I find that my parents, long dead now, still figure in many
of my dreams and that I think of them perhaps more now than
I ever did when they were alive, wondering what they would
make of me now, whether they would approve or be shocked.
I still live to please them, in a way, and I'm still surprised by their
reactions. Just as I was when they were alive. I remember that
when I became a professor, I was so proud, or rather so pleased
with myself, that I couldn't wait to cable my parents (you could
still do that in those days!). The reply was a long time in coming, but when it did, all my mother said was "I hope this means

that now you will have more time for the children!" I haven't forgotten. The values of my parents still live on.

It makes me pause and think, this whole tragic story, about how *I* will live on in the hearts and minds of *my* children and of those for whom I cared. Would I, I ask myself, have been as ready as Philip Lawrence to confront the aggressors, have been prepared, literally, to lay down my life for those in my care? How many people would want *me* back for Christmas? What reactions, what sayings, what principles will *my* children dredge up from their memories? It's a sobering thought, one to give me pause.

I pray silently, sometimes, in the dead of the night, in these troublesome times, that ancient cry of the psalmist, "Deliver my soul from the sword, and my darling from the power of the dog." Yet I know, of course, that death comes to us all, and sometimes comes suddenly, out of the night or on the highway or, sadly, on our streets. We must therefore, as they say, plan to live forever, but live as if we will die tomorrow. Because we don't disappear when our bodies go, we live on, I'm sure, in the lives of those we loved, and it behooves us therefore to have a care for what it is of us they will remember and what they will treasure. If more parents knew this in their hearts to be true, there might, perhaps, be fewer knives on our streets today.

LIFE IS NOT A
DRESS REHEARSAL

℘ Were you around at the time of the Live-Aid concert in aid of the Ethiopian famine victims? Perhaps you were there. By all accounts more people listened around the world than ever listened to a pop concert before, and they gave more money. I'm only now getting my mind around the number. The mere thought of organizing such an extravaganza, awash with egos and technology, still leaves me gasping, and I loved at the time the sight on my television of so many people having fun while doing good. I grew up thinking that doing good meant dark clothes and serious faces. But I think that what impressed me most of all was that Bob Geldof had had a dream, a great huge, colossal dream, and decided to do something about it. I dream of great ideas too, sometimes, though not quite as great as that, but then I think that if it was all *that* great someone would have done it already; or anyway it will be easier to do next year, when I've more time, or when the children have left home or when . . . or when. . . . But he damn well went and did it!

I remembered then my friend who suddenly announced the other day, apropos of nothing in particular, that she, at forty-five, had suddenly realized that life was not a dress rehearsal. Yet there I was, at fifty-two, still wondering what I was going to be when I grew up. It's a nice thought that old age is always ten years older than you are now, but it can lead to postponing the future till you end up as the man with a bright future behind him! Whatever happened to old so-and-so?

We all know people who live lives of deferred gratification, waiting till they're fifty or retired or just a bit richer to live where they want to live, do what they want to do, go where they want to go. How many of them ever get to do it? And how many of them, when they get there, still find it worth all the waiting and the striving and the saving?

Life isn't a dress rehearsal. The party's for real. Perhaps that is what is meant by Christianity's insistence that God became Man. Religion, God, heaven were not separated out but all mixed in with us on earth. Life wasn't an anteroom for heaven but the stage for heaven, should we choose to play on it.

Quite transforming it was for me, that thought. Stop compiling a curriculum vitae, it said to me, a list of jobs and roles, an obituary notice to show St. Peter; get on with living as if you were already in heaven. And heaven, for me, isn't harps and angels and fluffy clouds, but joy and love and laughter and, most of all, a sense of timeless being, at peace with myself and my God. You see it, don't you, in the faces of those about to die or hear it as I did in the words of my not-so-old friend recently. Given six months to live, he said he felt a much nicer person suddenly, all hassle over, all enmities forgiven. But why wait for death to taste of heaven?

So, *carpe diem,* as the Romans put it. Postpone your dreams no longer. One man *can* move mountains, or at least fill a stadium. Being good can indeed be fun. *This* play's for real, I reckon, so today, I say to myself, why not *be* what you want to become.

THE GOD OF SMALL THINGS

ℂ **A**mazing! They have given the Booker Prize to a book which I not only have read but which I hugely enjoyed. What a nice world it is when what is enjoyable is also commendable. The book, as you will know by now, is *The God of Small Things* by Arundhati Roy. It is a languorous, evocative story of a family in Kerala, in South India. Nothing out of the ordinary happens in it—people love or marry the wrong people, careers falter and wilt, the family squabbles, a child dies— but these small matters are, of course, the stuff of life, as the book chronicles so well.

Listening to the news each day, I often get depressed, not so much by what's in the news but by the message it conveys— a message of my own smallness or insignificance in the great scheme of things. Don't listen then, says my sensible wife; but I am addicted. It is either addiction or a form of escapism, a flight into a world which I can't influence but which allows me to forget for a moment the small things which I can do something about—finding a plumber to fix that drip, buying a birthday card for my sister, apologizing to my wife for talking over her last night at that supper party, writing a thank-you note to our hostess.

Small things can make a big difference. Those thank-you letters for instance. I was cut out of my great uncle's will, I later discovered, because I consistently failed to thank him for his Christmas check. My excuse was that my letters were so boring that he wouldn't want them, but now that I am his age I realize how upset I can get by the apparent ingratitude of the young, or even the old for that matter. There are other things too. Names, for instance. Once, early in my career, my boss's boss stopped by my office to give me the glad hand. "How are things, Bob?" he said. "And how are the wife and kids?" "Fine, fine," I replied, but inwardly I wanted to shout, "My name's not Bob, you stupid git, and I don't have a wife or kids." A small thing, no doubt, but I never really trusted him again.

It is the small things that measure our days and define our personalities—the relief when a toothache goes, the comforting scent of baking bread, watching a flower unfold in the sun, the light in her eyes, or his, at your approach, the way you greet a stranger, deal with the kids, cook the meal, remember or forget to ring when you're away. The devil is in the detail they say, but you can look at it the other way round. As my favorite mystic, Dame Julian of Norwich puts it, "God is in everything that is Good"—particularly, it seems to me, in the small things of life. It were well, then, that small should be as beautiful as we can make it.

THE WHITE STONE

⒍ United States presidential elections are strange affairs, I say to myself every four years, and remarkably long and boring affairs too. I suppose the rationale is that if you can endure a two-year-long election, you can endure anything.

The curious thing about the whole of the process is the pretense that one of these two men will run the country, alone. No one runs big organizations on their own these days, let alone countries. It has to be a team affair, although of course the man, or woman, at the head has an enormous influence. One would like therefore to know how good these two people are at running teams and, more important still, at picking them. It might even be sensible to elect the team and not just the leader.

Picking teams is not easy. If they are all clones or toadies of the leader, they won't work. Nor will they work well if everyone is the same sort of person as everyone else. They once staged a competition among a team of company chairmen, a team of trade-union leaders, and a team of students. They asked them each to build a tower with Lego bricks. The chairmen came last. They all of them wanted to talk strategy, which was what they were good at, not to do the actual building.

Teams need people of all sorts of types and talents. In management jargon we call them shapers, finishers, and evaluators and such like. St. Paul, I'm glad to say, uses a richer language when he writes to the Corinthians, talking of the different gifts of the Spirit and the need for each part of the body to make its own contribution. The point is the same, however; you need mixes of all sorts to make things work.

This may be a problem for the leader, who has to choose the team, but it's good news for the rest of us. Lots of mixes of talents and types mean lots of room for all our individual differences. To put it bluntly, there is bound to be a team out there somewhere, sometime, where our particular personality and our particular talent would help. Some find it early, some find it late, and if *you* haven't found a team or talent yet, then persevere.

When I doubt that myself, like every Monday morning, I get strange comfort from a peculiar verse in the Book of Revelations. "To anyone who prevails, the Spirit says, I will give a white stone, on which is written a new name which no one knows except he who receives it." It is that white stone which will tell me, I believe, who I really am and what I'm ready for. When I will get it, I know not. That I *will* get it I am sure.

RAT RACES
AND WHIRLPOOLS

I watch some of my students at the business school take on jobs which will, they know, require 100-hour weeks, all year, each year, cramming what used to be a forty-five-year working life into twenty or twenty-five pressurized years, and then what I wonder? I see others postponing motherhood until it is too late, and I have watched my son and his friends, these last three months, shut themselves up in a dark studio every day and every night until 4:00 A.M. to make their album. He is only twenty. There is more to life than just this music, I say. There is, for instance, the sunlight which you never see. He answers in the catchphrase of our day, there is "no alternative" if he wants to succeed.

I admire the dedication. I worry that they lose their balance, their way, and their sense of truth. What makes young bankers, I wonder, risk their careers for £3,000 profit on an insider deal when they know, they must know, that finance houses have their own sort of drug test?

Caught up each in our own whirlpool, what the *others* do quickly becomes the measure of what *we* should do, of what is right. In my world we call it "group-think." "You people," the Indian mystic said to me, "have lost yourselves in *busyness.*" I could be more dramatic and say that we are in danger of giving away our souls.

To re-find those souls we must learn to leave our whirl-pools from time to time, to withdraw and then reenter, refreshed and redirected. We need, I feel, to walk awhile in other people's worlds or, like the desert fathers of old, to go out at times into the desert and vomit up our double, the one that isn't us. We need, or at least I need, a regular place of stillness to reconnect myself with the God I believe is in me, my true me.

"Be still then, and know that I am God," sang the psalmist, but it's hard today to hear his song amid the din of all our doings.

THE DANDELIONS

ॐ "Am I wrong," I said yesterday, "or is the English spring one of those few things that gets better every year?" "You're just getting older," she said; "it's always wonderful." And wonderful, indeed, was the thing we were looking at—a long pasture of lush new grass, but now completely covered in dandelions. It was like a sea of miniature sunflowers floating on a cushion of emerald green. Incredibly pure and beautiful. And just the week before, I reflected ruefully, we had been poisoning all those dandelions which had had the impertinence to seed themselves in my lawn, interrupting the perfect symmetry of straight, weed-free lines. How can it be, I wondered, that the same dandelion could be one day a weed, the next a mini-sunflower. It's nothing to do with the dandelion, of course, but everything to do with me and the way I look at it.

It's not a private matter however. The way you see things does make a difference to the things themselves. Only last night my daughter was saying that when she worked in Rome everyone treated her as if she was beautiful, so she felt beautiful and, indeed, *was* beautiful. It works the other way too. When I read a harsh criticism, last week, of something I had written, I wanted to shrivel up like a sprayed weed. And if you don't feel like shriveling, you feel angry and revengeful, which doesn't help anyone either.

There are bags of research findings to show that if you treat people as flowers they blossom, but when you think of them as weeds they shrivel. And if you want people to listen to your criticism or advice, you must never, the research says, treat them like a weed. All rather obvious really, yet we still treat potential flowers as weeds if they disturb the nice straight lines of our tidy world.

We could do it differently. Yesterday, after seeing the dandelions, I heard about a project which deals with teenage problem lads, drop-outs from school whose talents seemed to lie mostly in nicking cars. The police rounded them up and took them to a yard full of old cars. "Now you've got to make a new car from the bits of these old bangers," they told them. "We can't do that, we're stupid." "Oh yes you can, and you will." Resentfully and reluctantly they started. As it began to dawn on them that they could do it, their self-confidence and self-esteem blossomed. They ended up with a car of which they could be truly proud. Time will tell, but my guess is that most of them will go on to blossom in life and won't need any more weed control.

The way we see people affects people. If that is so, and I'm sure it is, then it means that we each do have the chance to give our world a boost just by changing the way we look at things and at those around us.

THE LURE
OF THE ZEROS

ℬ One day a property developer walked into a friend of
mine's house and offered him ten times what he
had paid for it eight years before—more than he had earned in
his whole life so far and just for sitting there!

Yes, this was London and at a time when thousands in the
Midlands and the North could not get *any* offer at all for their
houses.

Then I heard of a young man being offered a six-figure
"golden hello" just to make a job offer in a bank rather more
tempting, on top of a whopping starting salary. Could he really
be *that* good when millions, as we know, couldn't get a job at
all? Those were the days!

And at the time, too, there was my young godchild, just
qualified with a good degree in engineering from a top university; she rang me to tell me of her first job—with a prestigious
firm of stockbrokers. "But what about the engineering?" I asked
after I had congratulated her. "Oh, no one can afford to be an
engineer these days," she said. "I'm getting twice the money
plus bonuses."

Temporary imperfections in the free market—that's what
they said they were, and they will correct themselves in time.
Well, maybe, but it takes a long time, and in the meantime can
such huge imperfections be right?

It's my friends that I worry about. You can't blame them or people like them for taking advantage of their luck. Money is *not* the root of all evil; St. Paul was careful to say that it was the *love* of money which was the problem. But I wonder if you really can see straight with all those zeros in front of you, still disentangle right from wrong, above all still be *true to yourself* in spite of the numbers. My house-owning friend is thinking of moving to a house which is quite out of character in a world where he won't fit. The banker may find himself locked into a ghetto, a slave to his job and a bore to his friends, burnt out at forty. My godchild, engineer that she is, may hate the wheeler-dealing but be too rich to leave. I hope none of this happens, of course, but I've seen too many people trapped this way into living a lie—the worst of sins St. Augustine said.

We can't abolish money, and I wouldn't want to. Indeed we need lots more of it. It is the fuel of civilization. The trouble is that when the fuel goes where it isn't meant to, it can get messy and dangerous. I just hope and pray that those who have the money can set light to it personally and that they won't lose their souls for the name of the game. It was this I believe that St. Matthew had in mind when he recorded Jesus as saying: "Blessed are the poor in *spirit* for they shall see heaven." Is there time enough, I wonder, in this busy money-world for the things of the Spirit? If not, then we should make time if we want to stay true to ourselves in the midst of the numbers.

FIFTY THOUSAND HOURS

ஃ "A job is a job is a job," said the trade unionist, "and there aren't enough of them; that's all there is to it." Unfortunately it isn't. Jobs aren't actually getting fewer, anymore, but they are getting smaller, and that's going to cause new dilemmas for business and especially for the good business which sees its workers as its continuing responsibility and not just as costs in the accounts.

Think of it this way. We used to sign on for a hundred thousand hours of work in our lifetime. That's forty-seven hours a week (including overtime) for forty-seven weeks a year for forty-seven years of life. Today more and more people are working thirty-five hours a week in offices for forty-five weeks a year for what may only be thirty-two years of their life (from, say, twenty or twenty-two to their early fifties). Believe it or not that works out to be fifty thousand hours. Without really noticing it we have cut the job in half, particularly for those young people starting work today.

Fifty thousand hours instead of one hundred thousand hours. That makes you wonder what we are going to be doing in the other fifty thousand hours and what we are going to be living on. It means that firms have to start wondering whether they are morally obliged to keep people on until they are sixty-five even if they don't need them anymore or whether they

41

ought to pay them the same pension if they leave at fifty-five instead of sixty-five, whether indeed any business can any longer afford to offer anyone a job and a full pension for life if that life is going to last another twenty-five years beyond retirement.

Maybe it's more fundamental than that. Maybe we won't be "retiring" at all, just working differently. I asked an old farmer near here what the difference was between farming at seventy and farming at fifty. "No difference," he said, "just slower!" We will work because we have to, for the money, and we'll work because we want to, for the companionship, for the feeling that we are needed, for the sense of worth that only work can give. It's just that the work will be different, and slower. Much of it will be part-time, for two or three days a week or at hours of our choosing. Much of it will be effectively self-employment, doing bits and pieces of work for different clients. Some of it will be for money, some for free, some for love, and some because someone has to do it, like the housework or the caring.

Good news or bad? Good news if you enjoy the work because in the end it is work of some sort that gives point to life. "All play and no work," to reverse the traditional saying, "makes Jack an empty boy." Eden wouldn't have been a paradise for long if Adam and Eve had had no gardening to do. But it's bad news if the work means more drudgery and more slavery, working only to eat. The challenge of the fifty thousand hours is to turn them into an opportunity for all of us to create a better balance of the different sorts of work and leisure in the last third of our lives, the Third Age. Do that and I'll be happy to cut the word *retirement* out of my dictionary!

MARATHONS
NOT HORSE RACES

The season of Lent should be a reminder to us to find more space for contemplation and rebalancing in our busy lives. "Not so," said one lady. She thought that the point of Lent was self-denial. "Self-denial," I said to her, "has been the bane of this society and of its religions."

No, I am not advocating some kind of orgy of self-indulgence, and, yes, I do believe that self-control is important. What worries me is the whole set of attitudes which implies that being pleased with yourself is somehow suspect, that being different is dangerous, that cold showers are good for you, that high standards mean lots of losers, and that putting people down is the best way to make them spring up.

To put it bluntly, if we really did love our neighbors as ourselves, most of our neighbors would have a pretty raw deal. Or, to put it another way, too much of our society seems to be designed to make most of us feel like losers most of the time, be it our examination system, our class system, or our organization. It's as if we were governed by the philosophy of the horse race, in which only the first three count and the rest are also-rans.

You know, it's just possible that the mass marathon will come to be seen as the most important social invention of our age. In those marathons, you will have noticed, everyone who

43

finishes gets a medal, and winning means beating your own target, not the other runners. Why couldn't everything be like that? In some Japanese schools every child gets a prize for *something*, and in the best U.S. firms you get awards for *trying*, not just for winning.

Does it matter? You bet it does, and I'll tell you why. When winning is so important but so difficult, the best strategy must be to at least avoid losing. So, lower your sights, keep your head down, and above all don't try too hard. That way, if you fail you can always blame your laziness, not your lack of ability, and you can explain the laziness by claiming that the game wasn't worth the candle. I'm afraid that where humility is the mode, then apathy is the mood!

It's crazy, isn't it? I mean I need to be stroked, psychologically and positively, by someone for something *every day*. If I'm not, I get depressed and my energy slumps. And if me, then maybe others too. No wonder we the British do so pitifully in the economic effort stakes.

It's not only crazy, it's wrong. We are each meant to be different, aren't we? We are each given a bundle of talents, as I see it, in trust, to be used to improve our bit of creation and the lot of others. To ignore these talents in ourselves, to deny ourselves, is to spit in the face of the creator. To suppress them in others is tyranny.

So, why not love yourselves a little today and then love others. It's not soft! And if you want a thought for Lent, don't give something up, take something on.

COUSIN MOLLY
AND DEGAS

℘ Cousin Molly died yesterday morning. She was ninety-six and suffering a lot toward the end, so it was, as one says on these occasions, a merciful release. But still, for us who loved her, it was the end of an era, a new hole in our life, another taste of finality, and one more time to stop and ask Is it all a waste of breath, her life, my life, our lives?

Well, just before we heard the sad news, we had been to the Degas exhibition at the National Gallery, the wonderful late flowering of that artist's genius, and there I think I found the suggestion of an answer. The beautiful oils and pastels you see there all came about because Degas felt a failure. When he hit sixty Degas looked back at his life and work and decided that it amounted to nothing. The vogue for his impressionist art had passed, and it all seemed, now, a flash in the pan, a waste of paint. Degas turned his back on life and retreated to his dark brown studio, determined to create, at last, something special, not for anyone else to see or buy, just for himself. But he died at eighty-three, evicted from his studio, blind, lonely, and depressed. Only now can we see, for the first time, the full glorious fruits of his last twenty years.

You don't have to be sixty and a temperamental artist to look back at your life and wonder if it wasn't all chaff in the wind. From time to time I take out my old appointment diaries and wonder who all those people were that I was meeting, what those committees were all about, and what, if anything, we achieved. Nelson Mandela, who arrives in Britain this evening, has seen *his* life's work fully justified, but he says in his autobiography that he wondered at times, during those dark prison years, whether he might not have done better to have been an ordinary lawyer, at home with his wife and family. I suspect that even Jesus Christ, dare I say it, felt a failure as he hung on that cross, such a short life, so little seemingly achieved.

It is not for us, you see, to judge our life and seldom within our own lifetime. Degas would have been astounded to see the admiring crowds around his pictures. Perhaps he knows, somehow. If not, no matter. His work inspires *us,* as does his example, the thought that life, for him, reached its full flowering only after sixty. What's all this nonsense about retirement? Cousin Molly was still cracking jokes and bossing people around, in spite of all her ailments, at ninety-six. *And* she got forty-two cards for her birthday last month! Life *never* ends, even with death. Rest in peace, dear Molly. Your life, *for us,* was worth it, *is* worth it. You live on in us.

ORGANIZATIONS FOR MASOCHISTS

Thinking about it the other day, I realized that some of my unhappiest moments have been in organizations. Somehow it seems to be quite respectable to do things in organizations which you would never do in private life. I have had people insult me to my face in front of my colleagues. I have had my feelings rammed down my throat on the pretext that it would do me good and have been required to do things which I didn't agree with because the organization wished it.

And then there are all those games which organizations play, the political battles over what we can spend, who works for whom, or who sits where or is paid what. If, like me, you're not very good at fighting your own corner, you can end up sitting in the little room at the end of the corridor, wondering what they're talking about in those meetings you weren't invited to, simmering with resentment and hurt.

In my worst moments I have thought that organizations were places designed to be run by sadists and staffed by masochists—and I'm not just talking about business, some of these things happened in the holiest of places with the nicest of people. Why is it, I wonder, that 90 percent of us choose to work in these odd communities if we have the choice? Why does it sometimes have to be so awful?

Well, it doesn't have to be like that. The best organizations to be in, it seems, are the busiest ones as long as they are being busy for someone else. The worst are those that are obsessed with their own innards.

You know how it is when you say "How do you do?" to some people and they insist on telling you, in gruesome medical detail, how they *do* do or, rather, how parts of them do not do, and you realize that they obsessed with themselves, neurotic, boring, and probably useless to anyone else. The interesting people are often the healthy ones, those who are so absorbed in other things and other people that they haven't time to worry about themselves.

Well, it seems to be the same with organizations. The healthiest are those which exist for others, not for themselves. Show me a business or a school or a church that is preoccupied with its customers or clients, determined to do its best for them and not just to survive for the sake of surviving, and I'll bet you that they don't have time for too many committees, for forms, for politicking or for nitpicking about mistakes. Those are the organizations which are fun to be in, which give you room to be yourself, to express yourself, to grow.

We all, it seems, need a *purpose beyond ourselves* to make the best of ourselves. When we lose sight of that purpose, we get obsessed with our navels, turned in on ourselves. St. Augustine said it was the most destructive of sins, but it's one that's easy to slip into, to be fascinated by our bodies and forget why they are there. The government minister was being shown around the new hospital and told the administrator how impressed he was. "Ah," the administrator said, "but you should have seen it before the patients arrived; it was fantastic then." They told it on the comedy show *Yes, Minister* but it has the feel of truth.

It may sound odd for a professor of business to say this, but I reckon that our organizations could do with a deal more loving, a bit more forgiveness, and a lot more faith in other people. Such things, however, in organizations as in life, are possible only if we feel we are in the grip of something bigger than ourselves and so can lose ourselves in others.

"Where there is no vision the people perish," said the psalmist. Quite so. And organizations too.

FIXED INTANGIBLE ASSETS

ℬ There's a new phrase beginning to appear in company accounts—*fixed intangible assets*. It turns out to be accountancy speak for people. The truth is they aren't always all that fixed, as we hear yet again today. It makes me wonder if accountancy speak is the best way to think about companies. Last year a friend of mine bought his son a company for Christmas. It wasn't a very big company, and I'm sure that his son will run it really well; but just the thought of buying a company for Christmas knocked me back a bit.

It's happening every day, of course, in the financial markets, but it's odd to think of a company as a piece of property which you buy and sell. For one thing, that property is full of people, and, well, buying and selling people does seem wrong, particularly if it's done against their will. For another, the buyers and the sellers—the shareholders—have often been nowhere near the place and wouldn't recognize its managers if they met them in the street.

To my mind it is unbalanced and unjust when one group of people, those outside, the owners, have so much power and another group, those inside, doing the work, have so little. It doesn't even make practical sense. A gentleman called Diororus Siculus put it rather well, talking of Egypt long ago when its workers were owned by the pharaohs: "It is absurd," he said, "to entrust the defense of a country to people who own nothing in it." It is as true today of our businesses as it was of Egypt. Why should people care for something that other people own?

The early Christians had another model. They called it *Koinonia*, a community with a purpose. They made it the basis of their lives. The individual in such a community is a member, not an employee, a resource, not a cost, and is not easily to be expelled. Those who provide the investment needed get their fair return and their security, but they do not own it. No one owns a community, any more than any one owns a family. The language does not fit. I know some businesses today that are run like that. There could be more. "I want to work *with* people," said my daughter, "not *for* people." I know what she meant.

Communities must grow, however, or they will die, and perhaps they deserve to die. But growth has different forms. Last year I was talking to the proud owner of a vineyard in California's Napa Valley. He was explaining how he needed to squeeze every cent of profit out of the operation. "Why?" I asked. "Is it because you want to grow?" "Of course," he replied, "you've always got to grow, but I want to grow *better*, not bigger. I want one day to produce the best wine in California. For that I need to invest all the money that I can and grow the best workers in the business."

I liked that. It made sense for him, for his people, and for us, his customers, and no doubt for those who originally financed his work community. Maybe we should have thought more about those early Christians when we made property not community the basis of our law for companies one hundred and forty years ago. Now, I know this: a community with a purpose, better not bigger, *Koinonia*, that's the kind of business I would be glad to work with—or even for.

LIFE'S OPEN QUESTIONS

ℬ Here's another one for the *Guinness Book of Records*. A fine of one million dollars *a day!* That's the fine which the U.S. Department of Justice wanted to impose on Microsoft for breaking an agreement and inserting its own web browser into its operating system for computers. Maybe you don't yet have a web browser and wouldn't know one if you saw one? Well, if the techno-gurus and Bill Gates are right, we'll all have one before long, and if we don't, then our children certainly will. Just think of it, all the data in the world at the end of your fingertips. The answers to all your questions for the cost of a local telephone call.

Bliss say some. Education transformed. Uncertainty removed from life. I'm not so sure myself. You see, there are two sorts of questions in life, closed questions and open questions. Closed questions have right answers, factual answers. Open questions don't; their answers will depend on your point of view or your priorities. How many miles is it to Harrogate, where I am today, is a closed question. There is one right answer, unless of course you are in Ireland, my home country, where they are likely to say, "Do you want the long road or the short road?" But what is the best thing for you to *do* in Harrogate is an open question. You can collect information on the possibilities, but only you can decide.

The temptation is to turn everything into a closed question. That way there is no argument and no doubt. By the time I left school, I was convinced that all the problems in the world had already been solved and the questions answered. The trouble was that the answers were concealed in the back of the teacher's book and not in mine. Education in those days was about getting the answers out of the teacher's book and into my head. A computer and a web browser would have saved us both a lot of trouble!

Unfortunately, most of life's little problems confront us with open questions. How can I persuade him or her? What should the strategy be for my part of the organization? Or, more important, what is right and what is wrong? And what do I want to do with my life? There will always be bad parents, bad bosses, and, I'm afraid, bad priests to tell you that these are really closed questions to which *they* know the right answer. *We* should not believe them. They are stealing our choices and cheating us of a life. Suggestions they can make. The answers are ours alone. Religions deal with the most important question of all—the meaning of life. This is an open question for each one of us alone to answer. Web browsers and computers won't help us here. What we need is the support of others to sustain us in our individual search for an answer and the belief that if we persevere, we shall find one in the end.

1/2 X 2 X 3

~~~~~ We should all, no doubt, take comfort from the fact that the trade unions and government and business have all agreed on their commitment to a full-employment society. After all, if that's what everyone wants, it shouldn't be too difficult to deliver it. There's quite enough work to go round if only we shared it out differently. "If only . . ."—ah, but there's the rub! Those who have the jobs hug them to themselves, like small kids with cake, *and* they want any icing that's on top too. "And why shouldn't they?" the unions might argue. "If we improve our productivity so much, aren't we entitled to keep a good chunk of the proceeds?"

It's a fair question, but one that society hasn't yet faced up to. Who should get the benefits of increased productivity? Should it be the shareholders or the customers—or us? Most of us, if we're honest, would like to keep them for ourselves if we are the people who did the work. But if we do that, then in the end there'll be fewer of us in there, richer maybe but working longer. On average, those who have jobs are working the equivalent of an extra month a year compared with fifty years ago, and there's still some way to go; the Japanese work 320 hours a year more than we do—that's equal to eight weeks a year!

It shows. When our Japanese friend took us out to dinner in Tokyo last year, it was a cold, wet night, but he wore no coat. I asked why. "I had to leave it in the office so that they would know that I would be coming back later tonight." I can think of some British friends who would do the same because Britain, too, has gotten more efficient, but we seem to have chosen to take the benefits of that efficiency in cash, not time. If we can, we would rather have more money than more time, and the firms collude with us. "½ times 2 times 3, that's my formula for efficiency," said one company chairman, "half as many people as we have now, paid twice as well, working three times as hard."

  · Great for the half that stays, you might think, but I wonder. I wonder if we are right to trade our time for money so readily. Time, after all, is God's great gift to us, and He didn't give us that much of it. If we sell it all for money, we might be wasting it. I don't want my tombstone to read "Here lies Charles Handy, he earned a million in his lifetime" because I know that ultimately I shall be judged not by how well I *sold* my time but by how well I *spent* that precious time.

  I know, too, that we won't solve the jobs equation until we start to pay ourselves in time not money, working less for less, but that means changing the values of the nation. In the end, isn't that what we really ought to be talking about?

½ × 2 × 3

BEYOND
THE MARKET

In 1938, when Chamberlain returned from Munich with his little piece of paper, T. S. Eliot wondered whether Britain was now anything more than a collection of banks and a decent interest rate. Given the attention we pay in the media to the questions of the financial world, he might wonder today whether we were anything more than a rather disheveled stock market and a slightly *indecent* interest rate.

Coming from a business school, as I do, I am well aware of the necessity for markets of all sorts, be they for fruit and cheese in an Italian village or for stocks and shares in an electronic one. They are simply the best way that anyone has yet found of putting an acceptable price on things. But we should be careful not to push a good idea to unhealthy extremes, or we may be hamstrung by our own invention. Money, after all, was made for man's convenience, not the other way round.

To tell you the truth, I find *all* the markets rather too exciting these days. Like many others, I suspect. My little portfolio of shares is not so little today, but who knows that it will be in six months' time. My net worth, as they say, is decidedly uncertain.

My net worth but not, thank God, my real worth. I mean "thank God" quite literally because I believe that it must ultimately be by His doing that I still *know*, in my heart, that I do have real value, no matter what the markets say. When the world depresses, that thought keeps me sane. I also cannot help but notice that the old cliché really is true, the important things in life *are* free; they are outside *any* market.

The birds were singing this morning, I noticed with relief. I didn't, couldn't buy that. Nor can you or I buy friendship or the respect of friends or the look in the eyes of your children. My twenty-three-year-old daughter astonished her grandmother the other day by saying that her parents were parents no longer but her very good friends. Her grandmother snorted in disbelief, but we were tickled pink. To us that is being valued, and that's beyond price.

I know, too, from bitter experience, that you can't buy a clear conscience. I still have bad dreams over something I did to someone thirty years ago. No money will rid me of that memory, only his forgiveness. I could go on. You can't buy, I hope, the love of the one by your side, nor truth, nor sincerity, nor faithfulness. That cannot be by chance. God, it is clear, does not need markets to tell Him what things are worth. Nor should we. Not for the things that *really* matter.

THE MESSAGE
OF THE CHIMNEY

🐦 I'm in Paris, and a strangely quiet Paris it is. Nothing is going nowhere. If they're not on strike here, they're stuck in a traffic jam. It took me two hours to go two miles yesterday evening. And this morning many of the taxis, too, have joined in, leaving me with no alternative but to start walking. *And* it's bitterly cold!

The strikes are serious protests about serious issues, but I'm struck, as so often on these occasions, by something much more mundane. People are once again talking to people; strangers are going out of their way to befriend strangers, allies for a week or two in their shared frustration. Parisian motorists, even, normally the most competitive of individualists, have been seen leaving notes in their parked cars saying where they are going and when they expect to leave in case anyone wants a lift.

Remove the technology of modern life, it seems, and we often start to be nice to one another again. Technology can isolate us, for all its benefits. It started, I guess, with the chimney. Before there were chimneys, we all had to huddle together in one room just to keep warm, master and maid, cowman and son of the house. Then some unknown genius came up with the idea of the chimney, and the social stratification of society increased dramatically as all withdrew into their own quarters. Central heating, which is, more truthfully, decentralized heating, made it worse, and now we have our walkmans, our microwaves, or, if we're really trendy, the Internet and e-mail. You can get by, these days, without actually speaking to anyone at all. Just the odd grunt to show that you're alive!

I liked the survey which asked teenagers how they laid a table for a meal. Did they put the knife on the right and the fork on the left, or did they put them both together? And 40 percent said one and 20 percent the other, but 40 percent didn't know! They had never sat down at a table together but had always, as they say, been grazers, helping themselves from the fridge and carrying the food off to their own corner to munch on their own.

If progress means that we don't need to talk to each other anymore, then I'm getting worried. You can't begin to love and befriend your neighbors if you never talk to them, and, vice versa, they can't love you. It becomes a recipe for a world of solitaries. But most of us weren't destined to be hermits. People need people to be truly people, as the Parisians, in spite of all their frustrations, are discovering again this week. "Try walking instead" was my motto for this morning, but perhaps the motto for us all this festive month might be "Turn it off, whatever it is, and try talking instead!"

THE FAMILY TREE

ઐ At least an election focuses our minds for a while on what kind of country we want and who we might want to run it. Back in our own lives again we might fall to wondering, as ever, what those lives are all about, what we are up to dirtying the plates every day only to wash them up for the next day.

I remember my father giving me, a year or two before he died, a brown envelope inscribed "family papers." "I don't think I'm ever going to get round to looking at these," he said; "you had better have it." Inside was one of those family trees going back several generations. You know the sort of thing—Samuel, born 1827 died 1881, married Ethelreda, with a line below connected to a small string of sons and daughters, most of whom had died before they were ten. What sort of people *were* Samuel and Ethelreda, I wondered; what did they do, how had they spent their lives? How irritating to end up just as a name on a family tree which my father never even looked at!

Then I remembered the last five verses of the Book of Ruth in the Bible. I don't suppose that they are anyone's favorite verses, but they made me stop and think. They go like this. "Pharez begat Hezron, and Hezron begat Ram and Ram begat Amerinabad," then another eight "begats" until "Jesse begat David," the very last words in the book—David, who was, of course, the great king. Without any one of those begats David would not have been. Without Samuel and Ethelreda I would not have been. Perhaps that, in turn, is my *real* purpose—to begat, in case in generations there comes a David, a great one. I mentioned this to a friend. "Of course," she said, "I've always known that I'm ultimately just a conduit for the future of humanity!"

It is not given to all of us to be begetters literally. But if I take the idea *metaphorically,* then the Book of Ruth reminds me that I have an essential place in the scheme of things, even if no one remembers what I did. I will not have lived in vain if I leave the place still intact for the generations yet to come, if I have perhaps even improved on it a mite. We're not doing too well on that score, at present, I feel, as I look at the crumbling world around me. It suddenly does not seem a trivial challenge, to be a conduit to the future.

I think that I would like to vote for a politician who saw himself or herself as part of that long chain laid down in the Book of Ruth, who is less concerned with being noticed or with making a mark and more concerned with our great-grandchildren still unborn, still unnamed, who will inherit the world we are so busy fiddling around with. As for me, I can and do take comfort from the thought that even if I earn no medals in this life, no grand obituaries on my death, that if in the end I am but a name and two dates on a family tree, I will still have been that vital link in the scheme of things, and, who knows, there might be a modern David, a new great king, somewhere down the line in generations yet to come, a future that would not have happened if I had not been.

A GRANDMOTHER'S FUNERAL

It's a lovely day here in Paris. I am here on business, but what matters to me more just now is that in one hour's time I shall be meeting my daughter off the train from Prague. She is breaking off her stay in the Czech Republic and hurrying back to England with us for her grandmother's funeral. It is the end of an era in our family and the end of a special relationship for my daughter and all her cousins.

A great character was our "Gongma" or "Gaga," the names the small grandchildren invented for her. She may not always have been the best of parents—who is?—but as grandmother she came into her own. Her brood of grandchildren will always remember her weird and wonderful generosity, particularly at Christmas. Who else would giftwrap a collection of pepper and salt packages left over from airline meals or the stitches from her last operation, but put a decent-sized check in the next package to be opened? They will remember her disapproving comments—"That dress is positively indecent." "Don't young men wear ties anymore?" "What sort of a job is that?"—but they will also remember the chuckle in her voice as she said it and the twinkle in her eye. They knew that she loved them to death, no matter how hard she tried to conceal it. They knew that she would always be there for them when they needed her, ready with gin and reassurance.

In the current debate about our families, particularly the single-parent ones, the separated ones, the divorced ones, we should not forget the grandparents. They can often be the rock of stability when the storms rage, the assurance of continuity and love. In all families, grandparents can know better than most parents how to condemn the sin but love the sinner. Because they look back longer they can look forward longer. They know that adolescence doesn't last forever, something which parents sometimes doubt! They know that success comes in many shapes and that happiness has no formula. They know, the best of them, what is important and what is passing.

Of course, not all grandparents are the best. But there are more of them to choose from. I only knew one of mine, but my children knew all four, and some children know great-grannies too. Today there are also step-grandparents and honorary grandparents, those elders without children who are often the best mentors to the next generation, their care and affection unhampered by anxious responsibility. So, choose your grandparent then, or adopt one. We all need one at least. "Miss not the discourse of the elders," said the preacher in Ecclesiasticus, "for from them you will learn understanding."

There is not much else that I know of in the religious tradition about grandparents, probably because there were not that many of them around. I would like therefore to amend the Fifth Commandment to fit our times. It should now read, "Honor thy grandmothers and thy grandfathers, that thy days may be long and good in the life which the Lord thy God gaveth thee."

Good families have grandparents to remember. When they go we miss them, but they leave parts of themselves behind, living on in their grandchildren.

THE HEART
OF THE MATTER

Recently I sat in the East Anglian cornfields and listened to the cuckoo. The apple blossoms blew like scented confetti around my feet, and even the rain smelt good on the sun-soaked grass. In the background the radio provided yet more remembrances of times past.

What a very different world it is today, I reflected, from that one which I can just remember fifty years ago. And yet, thinking about it, how much is still the same, thank God—the cuckoo, the blossoms, the idle chat around the table, love and marriage.

I say love and marriage because my niece and her husband-to-be were staying with us, getting to know the tribe he was entering, poor lad! They were talking about their wedding and their life together thereafter, teasing each other about their little habits, practicing at being a couple, as young lovers have done since time began. Oh, I know that marriages are often different now, but people still make vows to each other, even if it's under a waterfall or in a meadow and not in church, and they still *intend* to stay together and to love each other to death. Outward forms may change in every part of life, should change, perhaps, in the spirit of the times, but the heart of the matter remains the same.

Sometimes, I think, in the hurly-burly of modern life we can get bemused, obsessed even, by the outward forms of things, so much so that we forget the "heart of the matter." In my own life, I know that just keeping up with the paperwork and the necessity to get the money to pay the bills can fill my whole life quite easily—and quite boringly, if I'm honest. We need, just sometimes, to turn off the television, to get close to nature and those we love, and to remember, once again, why it is good to be alive, whatever government is in power, whatever problems the job may hold tomorrow, or whatever the news is on the other channel.

Only then, I find, can I turn my mind to the real heart of the matter, the reason for my existence. To survive, to prosper even, has never seemed to be enough justification for a life. After all, a cabbage could say as much. I believe—and I can't prove this, of course, because the point of a belief is that it is not a fact, it *can't* be proved—that there really is some point to my existence, even if I'm still struggling to find it. I do know, however, that it has something to do with love and with making things better, whatever that may mean, for the ones you love. Working that out can well take a whole life, although I have known some who did it wonderfully in a very short life. I know, too, that I need help to get me back to that heart of the matter. Churches and holy places do it sometimes, but so does a weekend with two young lovers in East Anglia.

BORROWING
FROM THE
GRANDCHILDREN

ஜ P olitical events and children are connected, or should be. Recently my wife took two photographs of a small boy in Africa. The first photograph shows his bright, cheeky, cheerful face—all hope and fun. The second photograph draws back a bit to show him full-length, standing ankle-deep in garbage, the garbage that fills the street around his home. If we are not very careful, before too long the garbage will wipe the smile from his face. He was in Africa. He could be here in Britain, although I would like to think that the garbage here is more metaphorical than real.

As I grow older, I am more and more conscious that we haven't done much to remove that metaphorical garbage from around the feet of our children. While we have busied ourselves with acquiring a better lifestyle, the world they are moving into seems to have lost some of its quality, and their preparation for it seems to be failing many of them.

Last month I was in an East Anglican church where, unusually, the ten commandments were read out in full. The second of them came as a shock. I had forgotten it. "Thou shalt not make to thyself any graven images . . ." it began. "Thou shalt not bow down to them nor worship them, for I the Lord thy God am a jealous God and visit the sins of the fathers upon the children even unto the third and fourth generations." Stern stuff! And those graven images, it couldn't possibly mean the engravings on our ten pound notes and on our credit cards— or could it?

I reflected that, until recently, we used to borrow heavily from our children and our grandchildren-to-be, without so much as asking them, in order to prop up our lifestyles. We don't put it that way, of course, but call it the PSBR, or, in full, the public sector borrowing requirement. The Americans, who until recently were doing it in hundreds of billions, call it just a budget deficit. It's the national debt, and it is our grand-children who will have to repay it one day. Maybe it's time we stopped borrowing from them and started to invest in them instead.

"Who are today the trustees of our future?" Kingman Brewster asked once, when he was U.S. ambassador here. I hope that the prime minister, whoever she or he will be next week, is going to be one of them, but we are all trustees of the future of our children and our grandchildren. That's parenthood.

I am left with those two pictures—the young lad in Africa and the graven image of our own materialism—with the words of that commandment ringing in my ears: "I am a jealous God and I visit the sins of the fathers upon the children." There is still, I hope, time to make amends.

THE AUTUMN CULL

৯৯ I discovered last week what they mean when they say
that chestnut trees are self-pruning. They mean that
huge branches fall off in the wind, mainly on top of my car!

All in all it has been quite a week for pruning—if you can
call it that. Decimation might be a better word; trees and share
prices toppling wherever you look. The autumn cull you might
say. I have even heard some people talk of it as God's own cull—
His reminder to the southeast of England and to the financial
community that riches guarantee nothing in this world.

Well, useful reminder it may be, but I don't myself believe
in that kind of magician in the sky, doing what my insurance
company used to call His "acts of God."

But I do believe in pruning. I notice that after its rather
dramatic bit of self-pruning, my chestnut tree is still standing.
Cut back to its essentials, it survived, while others all around it
tumbled.

It's an old message. Cut back to your essentials and you'll
be stronger, not only better able to survive the odd storm but
freer to take on new challenges. It applies to people just as
much as it does to trees and to share portfolios and to every
organization everywhere.

Get rid of the clutter of your riches, Jesus told the young
man, then you can be of some use to me. Be like the lilies, He

said on another occasion, uncluttered, they don't worry about the future; *and* He practiced what He preached.

But it's easier said than done, I find. Myself, I *like* a lot of clutter. It keeps me busy. If I'm totally honest, I admit that I often want to lose myself in busyness, and I suspect that quite a lot of people are the same. I guess some would say that we are lucky to have the opportunity.

Yet looking out now at my chestnut tree, stripped down to its stem, I realize why it is that people often come out of a severe illness with a much clearer perspective on life, dismissing now as unimportant all the little nigs and nags, unconcerned about belongings and possessions, living each day to the hilt, serenely impervious to the worries of tomorrow. They have been forcibly self-pruned, and I know I envy them.

The dramatic events of these few days have made me realize that it is silly to wait for the blows of nature to recall us to our essentials—silly and a bit risky. Better surely to take it in hand ourselves.

At one level that means getting one's priorities straight, giving time to the things that will endure, like our loved ones, long after bank statements and job titles have gone on their way to the bin. But at a deeper, much deeper, level, I am talking about a journey in search of one's soul. About that I know only this, that it is a dark and lonely journey but probably, in the end, the only one that we all should start on before the next autumn storm.

WHERE NO
PHONES RING

🪶 **D**oes money make people blind? Sometimes it seems so. I recently visited Silicon Valley, California. They don't make money out of money there, as bankers do, they make money out of sand, turning it into silicon chips and doing wondrous things with and to them. They really may be seeding the future in that valley, not just betting on it. The worry is that that future, too, might become a place for the blind and the self-obsessed.

Take one company that we visited. It is growing 40 percent every year, and its offices are spanking new, pastel-colored, the meeting rooms all in glass, and cubicles not offices to work in—no secrets now in the horizontal workplace! But the odd thing, the uncanny thing, was the silence. No phones rang. So no one spoke into them. In fact no one spoke at all, except in the glass meeting rooms. This is the world of electronic mail, where your fingers do the talking—on the keyboard of your computer. Telephones are out of date. You work where you want to work and use the office only when you need to. Your computer is your traveling desk, with its mailbox built in.

Electronic mail can be, I know, companionable and fun, but the silence of that "virtual office" was uncomfortable. It will, I fancy, be an odd world when we are all sitting in our cubicles, somewhere, typing not talking. I worry about it because I think that we need other humans to touch, to love, and to rub up against if we are to be truly human, and I don't think that you can really do all that electronically.

Ironically, it has always been part of the religious tradition that a withdrawal from humanity brings one closer to one's god, but this kind of electronic withdrawal hardly qualifies as a religious retreat! The appeal of Christianity to me is precisely the opposite—that God, truth, and purpose are to be found in the midst of humanity, not apart from it, yes even in the midst of our organizations. If, then, we take much of the human presence out of the organizations, we risk their becoming communities without a soul, places bereft of moral purpose, ready, in their turn, to be blinded by money or by selfishness. We must not let those chips do that to us.

VIRTUAL VILLAGES

ꙮ Not long ago in our Norfolk village they celebrated the first hundred years of our parish council. All the old minutes were on display, and the accounts and the photographs. What was fascinating, reading those old minutes, was to see how little seemed to change, in those days, year by year. Even the names stay the same. It was a community rooted in the land, where change meant a change in the seasons or growing older—more of the same only more so, but never, ever, different.

Truth to tell, I'm not sure that I would have liked it that much. It must have been quite boring at times, frustrating and claustrophobic, but at least you knew who was who and what was what. Life had a rhythm and a point, even if it was just to keep things going for those who came after.

It's very different now. There are few farmers left. The new villagers aren't rooted in the land. They are computer consultants, lawyers, accountants, writers, and estate agents, with the odd contract gardener or small builder thrown in. They don't live off the land; they live off their wits and their skills. Intellectual property, it's called, the ability to make something out of nothing. It is, actually, what the future wealth of this country depends on.

It's very freeing and exciting if you have it, this new sort of property. Your life is your own to fashion as you want. You don't have to join the parish council, or the parish church, if you don't feel like it. You can be invisible, even in a small place. But something's missing, all the same. If other people don't matter to you, then you won't matter to them. Being free can mean being lonely as well as alone, and then you start to ask, "What's the point of it all if it's only for me?"

I suspect, actually, that we are all villagers at heart, particularly as we grow older. The trouble is that the villages are disappearing. They're becoming housing estates, which is not quite the same thing, and the work villages, the old organizations, are evaporating, turning into boxes of contacts, with no loyalty one way or the other. So we must each make our own village. Some will still do it where they live. Others, like me, will make villages out of our friends and contacts, wherever—a sort of virtual village. That way we can all belong to something once again. But here's a snag—if you want to matter to your neighbors, they first have to matter to you. To get you have to start by giving. How strange that what I used to think was a soppy, unrealistic commandment—"to love your neighbor"—turns out to be crucial to survival, as a human being, in the information age!

BLAME IT ON
THE GREEKS

✍ "I can't stand those dark December mornings," I said
to someone yesterday. "But just think," she replied,
"how many sunrises you get to see."

"Oh, don't be so twee" was my gut reaction, although I
was naturally too polite, or perhaps too timorous, to say so.

She was right for all that, but very un-British. It really
isn't done to look on the bright side. Britain is the only country I know where a constant improvement in our standard of
living is always referred to as a relative decline. Only in Britain
is second best an insult not a compliment. Only here is the
golden age somewhere in the past. Only in Britain is it more
seemly to celebrate a close defeat than a victory. They had a
great party on the British yacht *White Crusader,* I heard, after she
was knocked out of the America's Cup, but we almost apologize when we occasionally win a cricket match.

Come to think of it, success is almost a dirty word in this
culture while even achievement sounds a bit pompous. I remember once in my youth, when I won a scholarship, I locked
myself in the school lavatory for three hours for fear of the teasing I would get! On a more elevated plane, companies in the
United States *boast* of how much of their success they pass on
to the community or to charity whilst we feel that such things

are best done, well, quietly, or by individuals. Too much bounty is too much boasting.

I put it all down to the ancient Greeks, who have been infecting our educational system for centuries. Don't get too bumptious, said the Greeks, lest you make the gods jealous and they strike you down. Hubris, they called it, or the pride that comes before a fall. Best be humble, or pretend to be, and keep others humble too. If your subordinate or your daughter does well just make it clear that she could have done better. Develop a league-table mentality so that only one lot ever wins and most feel more like losers; that way the gods won't be jealous. Oh, and remember, praise corrupts, so ration it. It's all very decent but very depressing.

I'd like to see us shuck off those ancient Greeks and try another god. One who is never jealous, who wants a world where everyone can win at something, who sets high standards but forgives mistakes; a culture where celebration is OK, where joy is part of life and heaven still ahead. It would be a quiet revolution, of course, but isn't that what life ought to be all about?

THE PENDULUM
PRINCIPLE

ℬ℈ For four years I lived in the shadows of one of England's loveliest churches, the Chapel of St. George in Windsor Castle, built in the same style as King's College Chapel in Cambridge and in the same period.

There were services there every morning and every evening and five of them on Sunday. I went to at least one and usually two every day, except, interestingly, on Sundays. What had happened, I wondered, to my adolescent determination never to go to church again?

I went because I wanted to, needed to, not at all because I had to. I had in my own experience stumbled across what Bruce Reed once called the oscillation theory of the Church. We live, as it were, on a pendulum swinging back and forth between activity and recreation. We need both. The pendulum must swing or the clock runs down.

Recreation however can be more than rest. Separate the word out into re-creation and it takes on a more powerful meaning, a sense of recharging combined with a touch of rebirth or newness. We should come out of the process not only refreshed but a little different.

We each need our stability zones to escape to in the hurly-burly of life. For some it may be the golf course; for some, paradoxically, the routine of the commuter train; for others, the garden or the pub. For me, for those four years, it was the Chapel of St. George, but it was, I found, a stability zone with shove!

The form of service, I discovered, had its own momentum. The words are designed to draw you in, pour balm and forgiveness over you, and then push you out into the world to "live and to work" to the glory of God. And it worked; I went in tired or depressed and would come out with new determination and a new spring in my step.

And that was in spite of not being allowed to join in the singing, which was, I used to think, the point of going to church. In the Chapel the choir did it for you, and quite beautifully. That released me, I found, to lose myself in the music, in the beauty of the building, in the mystery of life. "Being" there was as important as "doing" in that act of worship. God, as so many have discovered, is in the stillness of things.

I needed this re-creation every day, but never on Sundays because Sundays contained no work. For some the Sunday or the Sabbath recharging can last the week. Some may make do with a monthly shot. I needed it daily, and I wish now that I still had that chapel outside my door every morning and every evening. Chapels, however, are a luxury and even, perhaps, an unnecessary artifact. We ought to be able to use just the beauty of the morning, the quiet of the evening, the touch of friends, or the peace of silence to pull back, draw breath, take strength, and push out again.

It is the pendulum which makes the clock go round so the pendulum must not get stuck, at one end or the other. It is as easy to lose oneself in the busyness of the church and of its service as it is in the busyness of life. So "Swing, my people, Swing," as the singer said.

THE PENDULUM PRINCIPLE

77

GO AND HE
GOETH NOT

   The man in the Bible whom I have sometimes secretly
   envied is the young officer who told Jesus, "I say unto
a man go and he goeth and to another come and he cometh." It
has never seemed to work quite like that for me.

I suspect that the president of Russia would also envy the
simplicity of that officer's world as he struggles to hold his own
world together. But the president and the rest of us are going
to have to learn new ways because no free person should have
to put up with being ordered around today, unless they agree
with the order and with the person giving it.

It doesn't make life easy. Some years ago, in despair at our
inability to run the business school where I worked in a busi-
nesslike way, we accepted an offer of help from a successful
manager who wanted, he said, to leave his business and apply
his managerial talents to something different. He was put in
charge of the administration of the teaching programs and was
appalled by the disarray he found. He called a meeting of the
professors, but no one came! "Why not?" he asked me. "They
probably had other things to do," I said. "It's like an invitation
to a party, they come if they don't have a better invitation. You
will have to negotiate a date." He did and they came. He told
them his new rules. One of them said to him gently, "Richard,

you can't *tell* us what to do, you can only *ask* us and see if we agree."

"Oh, I see, it's participative management time, is it?" he said. "Well then *you* tell me how we ought to arrange things." "No, Richard," they said, "that's your job not ours; *you've* got to come up with a better idea and win our approval or persuade us that this scheme really is the best. That way we own it and will deliver it." He groaned, but learned to do it their way. He was surprised to find how well it worked, with less cost, less friction, and less need for checking.

What it all means is that if you are a leader or a manager you will have to earn your authority from the very people over whom you will exercise it. We govern only with the consent of the governed and manage with the consent of the managed. It is the difference between being *in* authority, as that officer in the Bible was, and speaking *with* authority, as Jesus is described by those who believed in Him. It sounds like a tiny change of preposition, but it means a huge change in behavior.

We should resist therefore the temptation to assume authority and the power that is needed to back it. That way lies management by fear, or by the secret police. Earn the authority instead. The founder of Christianity was, in the old allegory, tempted by the Devil to take the power to change the world, but chose instead to earn his authority the hard way because only in that way would it last. It is sadly ironical that some of the institutions that later bore his name did not resist the same temptation.

They had to rule by fear. They did not last. Dictators around the world today should take note. We in our own organizations and families should take note. Authority has to be earned, I'm pleased to say.

CHINESE
CONTRACTS

℘ L ast week we sold our fridge. I thought the chap seemed
very happy when he signed the check. In fact, come
to think of it, he didn't even try to bargain. Oh dear, I thought,
I've priced it too low. I've failed again. Or had I?

I remembered then my days long ago in Singapore when
I was selling lubricating oils to the Chinese. We used to celebrate each deal with a twelve-course meal—delicious. But it
was when I brought out the formal company contracts for them
to sign that they started to laugh out loud.

"Now why do you want those bits of paper?" they would
say. "What kind of contract is it if you need a judge and law
courts to make it stick?" To the Chinese businessman, you see,
a good deal was one which was *bound* to be self-enforcing
because both parties gained from it equally, and both parties
lost if it went wrong. Formal contracts were superfluous, even
a bit suspicious.

"Oh," I used to say, "it's just an old English ritual which
my bosses insist on." But it wasn't just an old English ritual;
it was an entirely different way of looking at the world. I was
brought up in that different way, believing that a "good deal"
was a deal which I won, where I came away with more than
the other chap and where, if need be, I kept him to his bargain by the threat of the law. The Chinese way, of a good deal

being one where both sides win, was a very strange idea, but it worked!

I can't help thinking about all this whenever the Americans start talking to the Russians again or when managements sit down with their unions or when my sadly divorcing friends go to talk to their respective lawyers. Which philosophy of a "good deal" will prevail, I always wonder. But I also come up against it myself every day, and not just when I'm selling fridges. Only last week I was also arguing with some publishers over a contract, I was negotiating with my daughter over the use of the car, and I wanted the neighbor to repair the fence—all "deals" to be arranged. Which philosophy should I work to? Would I boast about the way I had got it all my way, or would I be pleased that we were both pleased?

If you think about it, it's pretty fundamental stuff. After all, if a good deal means a deal in which both parties win, then "compromise" isn't something to be ashamed of; it's right and proper. It means being serious about the other person's needs and wishes; it means seeing things from the other side of the fence and sympathizing with their view; and you can't do that, I find, unless you like them, or try to.

"Love your enemies," I was told when I was young. It seemed daft, then, and not the way to go about winning. Now—grown up at last—I'm not so sure. If good deals, deals that work and stick, mean deals where both sides win, then you have to start by genuinely wanting him or her, or them, to win as well as you; and that's not a bad start to loving. What kind of world would it be, I wonder, if we all genuinely wanted our opposites to do as well as we did in every situation? Naïve? Perhaps, because mankind is fallible; but it's an interesting idea, it's been around now for two thousand years, and to the Chinese it's also good business. But it has to be bad news for lawyers!

CHINESE CONTRACTS

81

A TOWER OF BABEL

℘ I must confess that I don't always understand the nuances of what goes on in British government, and he who does not understand should pass no comment. But I can't help being reminded at times of that nifty story in Genesis. It's the one where God thought the humans were getting above themselves and building a tower to reach to heaven. "Look," said God, "they are one people and they've all got one language, and that's only the beginning of what they'll do. Nothing now will be impossible. Come, let us go down there and confuse their language, so that they don't understand each other's speech." And he did just that, and the tower collapsed.

The story of the tower of Babel is a warning to us humans not to get too uppity, but it starts with the truly exciting idea that if we could only sink our differences and speak with one voice, *nothing* would be impossible. That was exactly what Bill Clinton was calling for in his victory speech in Arkansas immediately after his election.

I went to the United States last year, invited to give a speech on the management of diversity. I thought that that was a smart word for change, which is my hobbyhorse, so off I went, quietly confident. But as I listened to the first two speakers, I realized that diversity is U.S.-speak for minorities, people of different races, colors, and languages. The *variety* of which the United States once boasted had become a problem of *diversity*.

As I frantically scribbled a new speech, I thought about that tower of Babel. Why had what Americans used to call their salad bowl of variety degenerated into a smoldering cauldron of diversity? I wasn't going to believe that they were being punished by God for being uppity. But you could see and hear it; their differences were beginning to be greater than their togetherness. I could not say that it is any different in Europe, or even in our little bit of Europe.

Differences should be a delight and not a problem. The strongest societies, the strongest organizations, the strongest marriages are those which delight in their differences but which can understand each other and can speak with one voice. The danger, the tower of Babel danger, is that the differences turn into *separateness* if they can no longer talk together because they lack that common voice. In Catholic theology, to be separate, to be cut off from others, is to be in Hell. Anyone who has *been* separate will know that.

It's my sense that, in recent years, our pursuit of individualism and tribalism, in both our countries, has brought us close to separateness, to the brink of hell. It has been a recipe for depression, both economic and personal. I now feel that we are drawing back from the edge. It's my hope that, delighting in our differences but with a common understanding, we may yet, both in Europe and in the United States, build something to make God take note.

THE "THEY" SYNDROME

∾ "They really ought to do something about it," said the taxi driver the other night, pointing at the traffic jammed up ahead of us. Who "they" were or what they should do was, naturally, not specified. It was just another example of what I have come to call the "they" syndrome after the woman who told me that she was having to move out of her married quarters with her child because she was separating from her army husband. "Where are you going to live then?" I asked. "They haven't told me," she said. "Who are they?" I said, curious. She looked at me as if I was peculiarly stupid. "They haven't told me who they are, have they?" she said witheringly.

I shouldn't be so scathing. I spent ten years in a big company waiting patiently for them to shape my life while *they* deplored my lack of gumption in taking no initiatives. And I'm often wondrously tolerant of expert authority. When the doctor told me that they knew nothing about the cause of my virus and could not cure it, I murmured "thank you," hugged my pain to myself, and went away strangely reassured that "they" were no wiser than me!

A proper deference, you might say. Sheer escapism is more often the truth, and it's very pervasive. Any organization will have its "theys" who, everyone hopes, are taking care of the future, although, when pressed, no one is quite sure who

84

"they" are. It does let the rest of us nicely off the hook; lazily, passively we wait, for someone else.

I think that a lot of it is all to do with religion, but religion tragically misunderstood. "Almighty God," we pray, and Almighty He is, but that doesn't mean that He's our general factotum, sorting everything out for us. No, the excitement of Christianity for me is its insistence that God became Man, that God works through us, that I can't leave it to Him, that He is in fact in me. Frightening when you think about it, but, actually, it's what gives life its meaning and its purpose. I would never want to think of myself as a predetermined doll, going through the motions in the hope of Nirvana at the end.

I suppose I take what's called a high view of Man—of mankind, that is. I go along with St. John, who said that the divine seed dwells in us, and also with Athanasius (he of the creed), who said, "He was humanized that we might be deified." I refuse to be what C. S. Lewis said I should be—a small, dirty object in the presence of God; that's where the "they" syndrome starts.

Take the high view and you give power to yourself, more things become possible, I find, problems turn out to conceal opportunities, blocks turn into stepping stones—well, most of the time. It's worth a go anyway, so why not believe in yourself for a change, and stop delegating upward. He doesn't like it, nor should "they"!

THE GREENER
GRASS

There is one very puzzling parable in the Bible, at least to me. Actually, there is more than one which perplexes, but then parables are meant to be full of meanings and I can't claim to catch them all.

Well, this is the one about the farmer who hired some people to work on his land early one morning. As the day went on, he hired a few more, and some right in the last hours of the day. Then when it came to pay them, he gave each of them the same amount, no matter how many hours they had worked. When the early birds grumbled at this, the farmer replied that he had paid *them* exactly what had been agreed and that if he chose to pay the same to the others that was due to the kindness of his heart and was no cause for them to complain.

When I first heard this story, I felt that Jesus was condoning injustice *and* arbitrary pay policies. Then I learnt that the parable was about the generosity of God's love. But parables at their best carry personal messages, and the message for me in this story is about the destructiveness of envy.

Some hold that envy is the spur to economic growth, and I guess that much of advertising is based on this belief. Dissatisfied souls try harder. It doesn't work that way with me. I want to pull down the others rather than climb up to them, just like the complaining laborers in the story, and when I can't, I growl and grumble about the unfairness of life until self-righteous misery envelops me.

I feel that way when I see the tables which come out every year in the Sunday papers comparing typical British earnings. If you saw one recently, it would have had Britain's best-paid businessmen at the top, with well over one million pounds a year, while professors and their ilk, like me, came a good two-thirds of the way down the list. Naturally I didn't linger long on those below me on the list; I looked spitefully and enviously at all those above me. Quite ruined that sunny Sunday afternoon.

Actually we don't even need the lists. Research shows that if organizations conceal their salary lists to stop people from getting jealous, then everybody makes their own guesses anyway about their colleagues; and they always guess that the others are getting more than they really are. It's a sort of envious masochism in us, and the result, I have to say, is seldom new endeavors, seldom an end to any unfairness, just more unhappy people, just like the laborers in the parable.

So I have now resolved some things. I will try not to begrudge others their good luck in life but will wish them well with it. I will stop wondering about what might have been if I too had got in on those shares, if I had not sold the house five years ago or left that job. I will not yearn for the grass on the other side of the fence, which might be greener but seldom is, for I know, in my heart, that it is easier to walk down life's path if you look straight ahead and not over your shoulder at other people. It is certainly less depressing.

FISH SOUP

I was fortunate enough to find myself in Prague recently. I confess that I had not realized what a beautiful city it was, but it is one rapidly sinking beneath a crush of tourists. It is interesting, incidentally, how it's always *other* people who are "tourists"; we ourselves are genuine visitors. But if you want ever again to stand alone on the Charles Bridge in Prague at sunset, then go there now. Before long there will be no standing space left.

It is understandable. The beauty of their city and of their countryside is just about all that the Czechs have to sell us at this moment—hence the tourists. It will all come right in the end, I am sure, for such a cultured, well-educated, and enterprising nation, but it takes time to turn an economy around, and a way of life.

A current Polish witticism summed it up rather well, I thought. "It is not so hard to turn the contents of an aquarium into fish soup; the problem is to do it in reverse."

Freedom is heady stuff, but it's also painful having to make all those choices and decisions. Sometimes it really *is* easier to be told what you can have and what you must do even if you don't much like what it is. As a friend there said to me, "Of course, we used to have these awful cars, but at least we all had the *same* cars, so there was no point in worrying about it."

Learning to be a fish again, swimming for your life in the big aquarium, is painful and confusing.

No wonder then that the churches and synagogues of Prague are filling up, with relieved but confused people. They aren't going there to be told what choices to make, or if they are, then I hope they will be disappointed. Churches are not there to tell you what to do with your life but to give you the strength to make your own decisions, the strength to live up to yourself. We are not puppets on a string from heaven but free spirits with the right to muck up our lives *or* make the most of them. It may not be easy, but I wouldn't want it any other way.

Returning to this country, I wondered whether we here in this society were an aquarium or a fish soup. A lot of people nowadays are having to learn to swim, often rather late in life. The organizations and institutions which they hoped would organize their lives for them are not now going to do it for so many or so long. We are all having to take charge of our own destinies, both economically and spiritually, just as in Prague. I believe *that* to be good news but tough news. We shall need help. Will *our* churches fill again? Maybe, if they change their ways a bit. And they might. Am I too sentimental in seeing a gleam of hope in the quirky coincidence that the early Christian symbol was a fish? In our beginnings we often find our futures.

GROUP-THINK

ast week I went to stay with my mother-in-law. Now mothers-in-law aren't for staying with in the myth, but actually I greatly enjoy my time there. Not only does she ply me with excellent food and drink, but I get to read her newspapers! That provides me with a very different view of Britain from the one which I normally get over breakfast. How strange to find that not everyone is arguing rationally about the Anglo-Irish agreement, economic forecasts, or the latest business merger. What odd interests other people have!

The truth is that it's very good for me to be bereft of my normal newspapers. I have to start to think for myself. No prepackaged opinions on the issues of the day are there to confirm my prejudice and tell me what to say. My comfort zone is removed. We are all quite good, I guess, at creating these comfort zones—not just newspapers, but friends who think like us. It's what makes life predictable.

In the jargon of my profession it is called group-think, a state of affairs in which all around are of a common mind so that no one notices that the emperor is actually naked, or at least no one would ever presume to say so. I shall always remember the fascinating research studies of the groups where all but one of the members are briefed beforehand to say that what is clearly the shorter of two lines seems to them to be the longer one, with the result that the one unbriefed member begins to doubt the evidence of his own eyes and will, in fact, usually agree with the majority!

It sounds bizarre. But it happens. I can think of too many times when I've nodded my head for the sake of a quiet life, when I've let myself be argued into agreeing to something which I know is wrong. A decent humility, you might say, or a respect for others. Too often it's just cowardice, or laziness—the comfort of group-think. Organizations are rife with group-think. Members not only read the same newspapers but wear the same clothes, tell the same jokes. They even glory in it, calling it "shared values." Shared values are great, of course, if the values are great.

But those shared values can also lull you into a sort of moral anaesthesia, where you find yourself agreeing too readily that the obvious way to deal with the fall in profits is to amputate a bit of the organization, that it's OK to fantasize your expenses because it's "the unwritten law of the firm," that you must cut yourself in on the action because "everyone expects it." Cocooned by like minds we can drift into a moral swamp, like the man who was amazed to find himself jailed for being what he thought was just a clever businessman.

Truth actually is important, I reckon; being true to oneself, that is. Living a lie does not feel good, and organizations which lie to themselves come to a distressingly predictable end. Best to remember the psalmist who reckoned heaven was for him "who doeth the thing which is right and speaketh the truth from his heart" or to go with George Orwell, who said that even if you are in a minority of one you aren't necessarily mad.

"Know yourself," said the Greeks. "Be yourself," I would add. It may not be comfortable. It has to be better.

GLOOMING
IN THE BATH

ஓ L ast Sunday the final hymn at our local church was
"Lead kindly light amid the encircling gloom." It
seemed rather appropriate, both for the Americans, as they go
to their polls today, and for us British, all of us looking for a
kindly light to lead us out of our gloom. We look in vain, I suspect. Governments, to their intense frustration, can't do very
much very quickly about doom and gloom.

If they can't, then we must. We can start by looking for
the bright spots, the bits that don't get mentioned in the news.
Yesterday, for instance, on this program, I heard that the British
Institute of Management had reported that women were being
blocked in their careers by the old-boy network. More doom
and gloom, and, yes, I'm sure it's true, but that is happening in
yesterday's world of big organizations, all pyramids and hierar-
chies. If I look *outside* those organizations, I find lots of ladies
pioneering in the *new* world of small specialist businesses and
independent professionals. No doom and gloom there.

Anyway, life is not all about work and economics, important though those are. Look beyond them, and in spite of doom
and gloom, perhaps even because of them, people still fall in
love, pass their examinations, watch their baby smile for the
first time, plant a tree.

Yes indeed, plant a tree. While I was reading all the doom and gloom at the weekend, a friend who was staying with us told us how lonely it had been in the early years of her marriage, shut up at home with four young children. To ease her gloom she lay in the bath and read endless catalogues of trees until she knew them through and through. She picked out the most beautiful of the trees, ordered them, and planted them around her garden. Today, thirty years later, her children are grown up and gone from home, but the trees are still there, to her delight, a rather famous grove of rare and beautiful specimens, while she is an internationally recognized dendrologist—that's the official name for a tree buff! It all started with glooming in the bath, but from the gloom there came another life.

So now I carry two thoughts with me to help me through the gloom. One is a Japanese haiku, a short meditational verse from the seventeenth-century poet Bashō. It goes like this:

> *When I look carefully*
> *I see the* nazuna *blooming*
> *By the hedge!*

That's it. But the haiku ends with two Japanese syllables, kana, which can't really be translated but are, I'm told, a sort of exclamation mark signifying joy and delight—"when I look carefully."

The other thought is from Mother Julian of Norwich, my favorite Christian thinker. This is what she said, and I treasure it: "He did not say thou shalt not be troubled, thou shalt not be travailed, thou shalt not be distressed; but he *did* say thou shalt not be overcome."

SUBSIDIARITY

છ A re you like me? Do you apologize to strangers for
    other people's problems—the traffic, the weather, the
state of English cricket? More seriously, do you yearn to take
over your children's problems and solve them for them? I do.
I've also tried to run an organization single-handed to save
other people their worries—and perhaps because, more honestly,
I thought I would do it better. And I'm not the only one. I know
people who attract other people's problems like a magnet; I
know managers who see it as their duty to solve all their sub-
ordinates' problems for them, and I know very caring people
who want to save their aging parents from any decision at all.

It's well-meant, I'm sure, most of the time, but I've come to
see that it won't do, most of the time. Stealing people's problems
means stealing their choices, and unless they are totally incapable,
that's denying them some of the responsibility that is their due.
The Catholic Church, I find, has a word for it—subsidiarity—
try saying that late at night! A papal encyclical explained what
it meant. "It is an injustice, a grave evil and a disturbance of
right order for a larger and higher organization to arrogate to
itself functions which can be performed efficiently by smaller
and lower bodies." If you didn't realize before that delegation
was a moral duty, you do now!

Actually, that's not quite right. Delegation suggests that you are taking part of your responsibility and giving it to someone else. Subsidiarity says that the responsibility is theirs in the first place and shouldn't be delegated upward unless they are incapable. It seems that giving away your problems and your choices is just as bad as shouldering ones that aren't properly yours.

Strangely, perhaps, it's often tempting to give away your choices. When I was in a multinational company, I was quite happy for them to tell me which country to go to and which job to do; that left me free to complain if I didn't like it. Indeed, I know organizations where problems fly upward like sparks from a fire, each layer passing the decision to the one above lest they get it wrong. And isn't it lovely, sometimes, to be given a problem, to be the expert, the responsible one, carrying the burdens of the world or at least of the family or the firm? And isn't it hard to say no, to say that the other person must decide, it's his or her responsibility, when you know that you could do it better?

I confess that I never find it easy to refuse a problem, but I've come to learn that it's often kinder to hand it back because it's only by managing their own choices that people learn to grow and be free.

The religious equivalent of delegating upward is, I suspect, "leave it to the Holy Spirit." Well, I don't know about you, but I believe that God also believes in subsidiarity, and while He is always there to support and inspire, He wouldn't dream of taking from us our right to choose. Choices, in fact, are our privilege, although they come disguised as problems, and stealing people's choices is wrong.

THE F'S AND THE P'S

The people of Russia are making the most of this, their sixth trip to the polls in four months. They may be frightening even themselves. They are, certainly, at best, ambivalent about the direction of the new reforms. I hope, sincerely, that they will continue down the road to a full market economy, but their hesitation is understandable. Capitalism, they must now realize, depends for its vitality on the right of the individual to be both different and unequal. That's not much fun if you are at the wrong end of the inequality.

The pope said, the other day, that he hoped that the peoples of Eastern Europe, in their embrace of capitalism, would not throw away some of the good things in the Communist ideal. He meant our concern for our fellow men and women. But there's something else too, as my friend from Dresden, in the old Eastern Germany, pointed out. "In those days," he said, "work was a place you went to, not something you did. The system was all hopelessly inefficient, of course, and it had to go, but it did mean that there was more time for Family and Friends, for Festivals and Fun. Now it's all about Productivity and Profits, Performance and Pay. Sometimes," he reflected ruefully, "I think that I preferred the four F's to the four P's."

It's the balance that we need, of course—both P's and F's. But last night I rang my goddaughter, who works in London's financial district, to ask her round for a Christmas drink. "I'm sorry," she said, "but I don't finish until ten o'clock on weekdays, then on Saturdays there is a pile of office work to do at home, and I sleep all Sunday." As a good godfather I should have referred her to the book of Ecclesiastes, where the Preacher reminds us that there is a proper time for everything, including a time for work and a time for the rest of life. I wasn't so pushy, of course. I wished her a good Christmas instead, knowing, however, that a Christmas full of F's is no proper balance for a life full of P's.

The trouble is that we in the West have made extraordinary gains in productivity in the last fifty years—yes, even in slowcoach Britain. That should be good news, except that we have chosen to take those gains in money instead of time, working ever longer and ever harder for more and more. A Faustian bargain, someone called it—selling our lives for cash. I would call it elitist idolatry. We have made a god out of work and then deprived many of the chance to worship him, hogging our idol for ourselves. Idolatry never did anyone any good. In the Bible, the Second Commandment is quite fierce about it, promising that the iniquity will rebound onto our children, even unto the third and fourth generation. Pursue the efficiencies of the market, therefore, I would say to my Russian friends, and eschew nationalism, but remember to mix the F's with the P's for your own sake, and that of your children.

WE ARE ALL
ALCHEMISTS

ॐ I t hasn't been the fall of the stars that has fascinated me at this year's Wimbledon but a message from court No. 8 which said, "The net monitor has broken down, please send a human." Is that now our role, I wonder, to be the fall-back in the electronic age? It's rather like when you telephone some institution and are asked to press one for this and two for that and, then, in a rather condescending way, are told to hold on if you want to speak to a real person, implying that you are a bit of a failure if you haven't been able to sort out your problems without human help.

If the modern world can increasingly do without humans, and all their fallibility and expense, what are we all going to do? Press buttons on telephones all day long? It doesn't sound much like Nirvana. But perhaps we should be very un-British and look on the bright side for once. Boring work will increasingly be done by machines. What, after all, is so thrilling about watching a net at a tennis match all day long, even if it is at Wimbledon? Maybe we were meant for greater things. The exciting thing about the future is that the new wealth is going to come from making something out of nothing. Writing a software program consumes no raw materials and contaminates no environment. The new product, the program, comes from nothing, out of the head of the programmer. Or suppose you dream up a new service, like the young man around the corner from us who will collect your clean laundry, iron it for you, and bring it back that evening. It's new wealth out of nothing, the alchemist's dream come true, gold from the ordinary stuff of life.

The trouble is that these new products and services have to be created by ourselves alone; they don't come from big corporations who are busily replacing their humans with electronics. And the problem with that is *us*. Most of us don't feel that we can do it. Who me? we say. I'm ordinary. I'm a responder, not a starter. Unfortunately, I think that the starting habit has been bred out of most of us, and we shall have to start breeding it back in or we shall all be both poor and idle.

It is, in the end, a matter of what you believe about yourself. Nelson Mandela, who is visiting Britain next week, said, "Our deepest fear is not that we are inadequate. Our deepest fear is that we are powerful beyond measure. It is our light, not our darkness, that most frightens us. We ask ourselves, who am I to be brilliant, gorgeous, talented and fabulous? Actually who are you *not* to be? You are a child of God. Your playing small doesn't serve the world. There is nothing enlightened about shrinking, so that other people won't feel insecure around you. As we let our light shine, we unconsciously give other people permission to do the same." Amen to all that, I say. We must not be afraid to be wonderful.

A HOLY PLACE

The traffic in London was terrible. Everyone was late for everything. No matter that some terrorists had tried to blow up a bank. We were determined to press on with the minutiae of our own little lives. In fact, it is just when life seems particularly random or pointless that we often rush to take refuge in the ordinary things. To stop and wonder what it's all about seems too frightening and too threatening. And yet, in the hurly-burly of life today, it can sometimes be wonderfully refreshing to do just that, if only we knew how.

I got a clue of what that might be when we were in Italy last month. Jenny, our friend, took us to lunch in the country with Freid. "You'll enjoy Freid," she said, "and the food is sure to be good, but . . . I want to show you something special there." Freid *was* fun, and so was the food and the wine, and I was composing myself for a siesta when "Would you like to see the church?" said Jenny. A church? The place was in the middle of the fields, far from any village, not a church in sight. But Freid's farmhouse, Jenny explained, was really an old monastery, leased to Freid by the monks. However, the monks still used the chapel at the back.

Jenny took us round and unlocked the door. We walked into another world. The chapel was still, cool, dark. When our eyes adjusted to the dark, we saw that it was very plain and very simple. Bare white walls, a few chairs, a stone altar, and a crucifix. It was six hundred years old, maybe seven hundred. You knew instantly that this was a place where people had been praying for centuries. It was a holy place.

No one spoke. Words would have been a sort of sacrilege. We were each left alone with our thoughts. I thought how, suddenly, all the trappings of the world outside had dropped away. My things, my ambitions, the books I write—what did they matter in this place? I was stripped down to my essentials, to just "me." Very frightening. But then the reassurance started. I could at least *wonder*, wonder not least at those monks who had been content to live out their lives and leave no mark behind, not even their own birth names, in the service of what they believed. I could *love*, too, I realized, even, occasionally, love others more than myself; and, in this place at least, I could face up to the *truth* about myself and resolve to live more fully to that truth.

Standing there, no, kneeling by now, I felt strangely at peace, at ease with my stripped-down self. I had rediscovered wonder, love, and truth, the essence of life and of all religions. It is precisely when life gets too complicated and seems too fragile that we need to be reminded, on mornings like this one, that there are some certainties, that there is some point. Now I knew why many old Italian farms had a tiny chapel in their midst. A holy place. Just to remind.

LAND MINES AND LOTTERY TICKETS

Land mines and lottery tickets do not, on the face of it, have much in common, but a visitor to my home recently reminded me that, in an important way, they do. One of the best-selling books of the moment, he told me, particularly in the United States, where CNN is making a film out of it, is called *Children at War*, produced and published by the Save the Children Fund. It is a description of what happens to children when their elders start their war games or, more alarmingly, after the war games have ended and the guns and the warriors have moved on. For then the children come out to play, and they fall on the land mines, with grotesque and horrible results. And if you ask who makes these land mines, you won't be particularly surprised to hear that the land-mine business is a profitable little part of *our* economy, creating quite a few nice jobs. Maiming children by remote control, however, is not, to my mind, part of a decent and a civilized society, no matter how much money it makes.

Lottery tickets are not, I'm happy to say, in the same league as land mines, but there, too, the unthinking pursuit of money can, sometimes, maim ordinary people and muddy the conscience of society. There is, these days, a growing body of research on the link between happiness and economics. Loads o' money, it seems, seldom makes us happier. I came across a club in California once called the Doughnuts—middle-aged people going nuts from too much dough which they hadn't earned, landed on them by their deceased parents, bringing with it problems and responsibilities that they could well do without. When we were first married, I asked my father-in-law for a small sum of money as a deposit on a home of our own. He refused. "You'll thank me one day," he said. "It's the things you earn in life that you will value, not the things you were given." Thirty years later, I have to agree with him. And what makes people seriously miserable, the research shows, is the inability to earn your own money and so control your own life—that is, unemployment. Work and education, not dollops of money, are what people really want to make them happy.

When it started, I thought that the lottery was a bit of harmless fun, a sort of voluntary tax, which might even do a bit of good somewhere. I never imagined, nor, I suspect, did anyone else, that the sums would be so gross. Surely it can't be right to hand out so much to so few when so many have so little. Apart from anything else, it makes money into some sort of god, when, in truth, with those sorts of sums, it is more like the devil. Some things, I think, I *know*, are more important than money. I would be prouder of this land I live in if we stood up and said that from time to time. We could start by banning the making of land mines and putting an end to huge bonanzas. It would be good to think that we did something because it was right and not just because it made economic sense.

QUALITY

I need to tell you about Richard, my friend. Richard was recently made head of a decent-sized business. "One of the first things I did," he told me, "was to gather all the workforce together. I told them that I was not going to stand for second-class work going out; we had to produce quality, to be the best. I expected grumbles, but instead they almost started to cheer." "You can't imagine," they told him, "how ashamed we have been in the past of some of the stuff we have sent out of these doors, but we were always told that we could not afford to do it better." "I'm telling you," he said to them, "that we can't afford *not* to do it better." "OK," they said, "but you'll have to get better presses than this one; can't do top-quality work on inferior machines." "Point taken," he said, "but give me time. It will take time."

I found it a heartwarming story because I have always believed that no one in their heart of hearts *really* wants to do shoddy work.

But of course quality does take time to work, time for the customers to come back again, time for the word to spread. And it takes courage: courage to sit out that first dip in profits, courage to hold the investors at bay, courage to outface the doubters and the faint of heart.

Still, this isn't meant to be a lecture on good business practice. I told the story because it seems to me to get to the heart of the human condition.

Quality, doing what you know is the best, what is the truth, will always work in the end *if* you stick with it and if you will give it time. The second best always turns out to be unsatisfying and, ultimately, unsustainable. "I passed, didn't I?" I said, crossly, to my headmaster once. "You passed, yes," he said, "but it wasn't your best, and you'll regret it." Silly old fool, I said at the time. Now I know better.

The great religions, at *their* best, have always known better. They don't think in five-year plans but of eternity. They know that quality, the right way, the truth, will prove itself in the end if, and it's a big if, enough people practice it always and without fail. They also know that they personally may not live to see the results. No matter.

Jesus knew this, even if some of His disciples didn't. Great scientists, great artists, and great leaders know it; so do very ordinary people, like my father I think, unappreciated by me in his lifetime, but, thinking about him now, I understand that he stood for quality and truth, and he remains a greater influence on me now than when he lived.

Most of us are "ordinary"—but quality, the truth, our best are always possible. It's just difficult. Very difficult. Why bother? Faith, I suppose. Faith that this is actually our purpose in life. You could say, "It's the will of God." That's all. That's enough.

WHO NEEDS WHIPS?

That was, you might say, an interesting night in Parliament. But it must be an awful job to be the party manager, I thought, as I listened to all the number crunching of possible voters and abstainers leading up to last night's dramatic division. And what an odd name it is that the British give to the job, too—a whip! The visitor from Mars would be bemused to learn that the worst punishment a prime minister can hand out to a rebellious follower is to withdraw the whip. Is it some sadomasochistic club you run down there? he might ask.

In fact, of course, far from punishing his rebels, the prime minister set them free, free to choose. If we exchange the language of fox hunting for the gobbledygook of management-speak, he unintentionally empowered them. And empowerment is infectious; it spreads to others, as the Government discovered to its cost last night. That is one of the great paradoxes of democracy, in the workplace and the home as well as in Parliament. If you empower individuals, as democracy would have us do, you lose control. If you trust people to make their own decisions, they sometimes make decisions which you do not like. No wonder those in charge have mixed feelings about democracy.

In the world outside government, the real world, it is no different. *All* of us are fully empowered, from the start of life, by virtue of our being human. That turns out to be the best-kept secret of all religions. We can and should decide for ourselves what to think and do and be, as soon as we are able, but the religions want their whips, because religions, like governments, want control. For whips read priests, preachers, and creeds of all persuasions. Every religion wants to keep its followers in line, for ranks of obedient followers carry clout. And lots of us collude with them. We *like* the whip. It saves our having to make up our own minds, even if we do sometimes find ourselves agreeing to things we do not really mean. In this sense, religions can actually *dis*empower their followers.

I find it encouraging, therefore, *not* depressing, that more people these days, particularly the young, are refusing the whip in their lives, are wanting to work things out for themselves, to find their own source of spirituality, and to be responsible for their own destiny. Some of us left it too late in the past. Arthur Grimble, who wrote a charming autobiography about his life as a colonial officer in the South Pacific, said that if he was honest, he had worked all his life to please the uncles. Then he woke up one day and realized that all the uncles were dead, long ago. Something of the sort happened to me. Now I know that I have to be true to myself and my conscience; I can't hide behind rules made by others. It's frightening at times, but also exhilarating because living a lie is some sort of hell.

ENTREPRENEURS ALL

꧁ I revel in my Irish ancestry and take every opportunity to go to that lovely country. Last year my wife and I found ourselves in the Irish Midlands, in the bog country. We stayed Sunday night in one of those lovely dilapidated Georgian houses in the middle of the fields which had been turned into a guest house by an enterprising young couple. But when we came down the next morning to the promised Irish breakfast, there was no one there. The shutters were drawn, the rooms all dark and empty. Our innkeepers had overslept! Undismayed, we raided their fridge, made some tea, and had our breakfast, the lady of the house appearing just as we were leaving, billowing with apologies. "We had a lovely night, and we overslept," she said, and, of course, we forgave her.

It was all pleasingly Irish and rather appropriate because we were going to a conference on do-it-yourself business, or entrepreneurship. One of Ireland's largest employers was planning to turn most of its workers into independent businesspeople, selling their product back to the firm but as entrepreneurs, not employees, responsible now for their own destinies. It is happening all over.

"Great," said some, rubbing their hands at the prospect, but others looked glum. Freedom and responsibility, even for oneself, can be frightening. I know how they felt, those glum ones. I used to be an in-tray person myself once, a cog in someone else's machine, useful I hope, but passive, not fully alive and certainly not in control of my destiny. But that was how things were meant to be, I felt, and I was not one for rocking the boat, not in those days anyway.

Then one day I read the first chapter of Paul's letter to the Galatians. In it Paul tells the Galatians that when he had his blinding vision on the road to Damascus, he went straight off to Arabia to preach to the gentiles, without speaking to any human being, and he did not check in to Head Office in Jerusalem for fourteen years, apart from a brief private chat with Cephas after three. "What I write is plain truth," he says, as if they wouldn't credit it. "Before God I am not lying."

They would not have put up with him in my company, I thought. And then I reflected, if Paul, why not me? But then I would have checked in to Jerusalem and been given an in-tray to deal with or, on Paul's previous record, would probably have been shown the door. Paul just got on and did it because he felt he had to.

In that sense Paul was, I think, the true entrepreneur, for entrepreneurs don't just belong in business. They are all the people who make things happen and don't just wait for them to happen in *all* parts of life. People like us, potentially. God may not speak to us as vividly as He did to Paul, but I believe that each one of us has something that we are meant to do, some difference that we are meant to make, somewhere. When we know what it is, we cannot wait around for things to happen; we should *make* them happen. As Paul did. As entrepreneurs do.

SIMPLE IDOLATRY

  "It is simple idolatry," said the man at the bar; "that's all it is." Actually, I think he meant *idleness* because he was banging on about the iniquity of the great Christmas/New Year shutdown, which grips the British nation once a year; although of course he *may* have been making a rather subtle theological point about pagan festivals, graven images, and so forth. Whatever he meant, it set me thinking.

Is it idleness, this long holiday, I wondered, and is it all decadent—the sign of a nation in the last stages of decline, the final collapse of the work ethic?

I'm not so sure. I don't believe that we are now so much less virtuous because we no longer work eighty-hour weeks in miserable fields and factories, no longer take just one day off for holy days and none for holidays or drop dead where we work instead of retiring. It is not *long* work that God and Calvin wanted but *effective* work.

Indeed it is my dream that one day in this land of ours we could have more because we produced more. It wouldn't require an economic miracle, just a lot of efficiency. If that were to happen, then the Christmas break would be a sign not of decadence but of civilization, a reminder that life was never intended to be all work and certainly not all paid work.

Recreation, better pronounced re-creation, has to be part of that fuller life. Even God rested. But we also need the other sort of work, the work we do for free and I hope with love: tending children, minding houses, caring for neighbors. Gift work is the pleasing term they use. To Thomas Aquinas, it is the best work.

Sadly, right now, the parts have separated out. Some there are who have too much time for recreation so that it is anything but re-creation. We call them unemployed. Another lot gets all the gift work—UDWs they're called; yes, Unpaid Domestic Workers, an accurate title you might agree, all those of working age who choose not to seek paid work. Honored of God they may be, but they go unrecognized by society although there are over five million such in Britain today. *They* might well say that gift work carried to extremes is no gift any longer but a chore.

And then there's all the paid work, with ever fewer people working even longer hours instead of the other way round. It was Mark Twain who once said, ironically, that if work was such hot stuff, the rich would have hogged it long ago. They have, Mr. Twain, they have.

Pray God, I say, for a blending machine. A separated society will soon go sour. Man that is made in God's image needs a taste of each of those three parts—paid work, gift work, and re-creation. When that has happened, for each and *all* of us, then, and only then, can we truly say that our Christmas break is a *just* reward for a just society.

SIGN IT!

ᗡ I was pleased to see an advert for a smart Swiss watch the other day, not because I need a smart Swiss watch (the cheaper the smarter these days, isn't it, in watches?) but because the advert said that the watch would come with a signature on it, the signature not of the customer but of the man or woman who made it.

That's nice, I thought—the worker has a name at last—because I remembered that when *I* started work my office door had the name of the department in metal screwed into the wood, but just below it was a slot with a plastic slip which you could slide in and out. My name was on the plastic slip. It was quite obvious, even to me, that it wouldn't make much difference to the door, the office, or anyone if someone else's name on another slip of plastic was slipped into that slot. I was discovering the real meaning of the sociological term *role occupant*. I was the human being who for the time being was filling that role. I wasn't really or fully *me;* I was the inheritor of a job description.

Now I know well enough that you can't run an organization without defining the jobs that need to be done, setting out areas of responsibility and patterns of accountability. Those are all essential. But it's wrong, morally wrong, I believe, to treat people as if they were interchangeable human parts. They aren't completely interchangeable. It does make a difference which name goes into that slot in the office door. We know it does. We shouldn't pretend it doesn't.

It's pervasive, this role-occupant stuff; that's what worries me. "What do you do?" we ask people at a party, but we don't really want to hear everything they do; we want to hear the name of their role, their job title, their organization—then we've got a box to put them in and the exchange of pleasantries can continue without anyone really getting to know anyone. Roles, job titles, organizational boxes can in fact be devices to stop people knowing each other, sorts of shields which we carry around in front of us.

It used not to be like that. The worker was a craftsperson or artisan; there was a signature of a kind to everything, whether it was made by the carpenter, shaped by the blacksmith, or tended by the gardener. Maybe, helped by the new technology, the tradition is creeping back, as with my watchmaker or with the credits on the TV programs which list all the names of the people involved. It does make a difference, having a name. One of the nicest things about writing books, I find, is having your name on the front.

It means that I have signed my work, and what I sign for I'm responsible for and accountable for. Signed work tends therefore to be better work. It's more important than that. Putting names before job titles means that we expect the name to make a difference to the job, and that's what we were all born for, to make a difference to this world of ours, we hope for the better.

There ought to be a law forcing each of us to sign our work. On second thought, why do we need a law when it's so obviously sensible and right?

THE CHOIR OF MALE CONVENIENCE

🐝 When my son was young, he had the dubious privilege of attending a choir school. It was dubious, I felt, because on top of all his schoolwork he had to do two and a half hours every day of music. It was hard work although he seemed to enjoy it.

After a bit I had cause to remark on a strange discrepancy in his end-of-term reports. Those from his form master spoke of his generally disruptive behavior, lack of concentration, and apparent inability to learn. The choir master, however, was full of praise for his diligence and hard work.

I spoke to the choir master. What was his great secret, I asked. Did he beat them or threaten to lock them up? "No," he said, "I do nothing. But I tell you what the difference is: in the choir they are doing proper work, with adults, and so they behave like adults."

It was a message that more teachers should learn, I thought, but I went on to wonder why it was that only in a choir school do young boys get treated as men. Then I hit on it: the only thing that grown men cannot do better than small boys is to sing in a treble voice. They have to let them in on the act, and if not small boys then soprano-voiced ladies.

Choirs are the necessary exception, it seems. Everything else has, for a long time, been organized for adult male convenience. It is very convenient, is it not, that one should have a work-home-from-home that requires our presence just for those forty or fifty hours when homes need cleaning and kids need caring. Inevitably it is a custom which excludes one person from that work-home, and there are no prizes for guessing which person that is!

I wonder, today, how necessary it is that we should all be in the same place and all at the same time in order to get the work done. I don't wonder, actually, I know that now most of us are assembling or processing bits of information not bits of things, and it is far from essential to be all together all the time, even though we shall probably always want and need to meet our colleagues two or three times each week. You don't have to have huge office blocks full of commuters to make *that* possible. But I do wonder when we shall get round to acknowledging that a lot of that office time had always to do with male convenience. I bet that we males would not have organized things that way if it was we who had also to run a home and take the kids to school.

Ironically, I think that if we started to organize things for female convenience, with more flexibility, more control over where and when one did one's work, more personal responsibility and less minute-by-minute supervision, men might actually like it just as much as women. Well, we shall soon find out because our organizations are going to need those women more and more.

Personally, I think that organizations of male convenience have always been unnatural, in every sphere. The myth of Genesis, as I understand it, was that Adam on his own would have been a nonviable operation, or short-term at best. I think that's still true.

LEARNING FROM
MISDOING

β Well, at least we've got Super Tuesday in the States
out of the way! One more hurdle jumped, it seems,
for George Bush and for Bill Clinton. But there are quite a few
hurdles yet to come, and, remember, this is only the first round!
Sometimes I wonder how anyone can have enough energy left
after such a dreadful marathon to even *think* of trying to run
that country as its president. Like many people, I guess, I wonder why the Americans still do it this way. It doesn't seem to
have much to do with the policies of the candidates, more with
finding out what sort of person each one is.

But then they seem to want their chosen candidates to
have lived a life without blemish. No peccadillos, no adolescent
experiments, no switches of policy, no bad marriages, and, of
course, no traces of illness. Yes, I know and they know that
most of the greatest U.S. presidents were either crippled in
some way or naughty, or both, but they still want a candidate
without blemish from birth. And yet I know, and they must
know, that a man without blemish is not only likely to be a
great bore but also someone who can have learnt little along
the way, for it is by suffering that we grow and by mistakes that
we learn.

The other day I was asked to take part in a radio series.
The idea was to ask a selection of people, one a week, to be

116

interviewed about what they had learnt in life and how and when they learnt it. Flattered as ever by the attention of the media, I agreed to be one of those interviewed. It was only when I put the phone down that I realized that I wouldn't be talking about courses and schools and colleges, that if I was going to do it honestly I would have to reveal it *all*, my big mistakes, my failures, the times I let people down or, God help me, deceived them and was then found out, or sometimes not. Will I (because it hasn't happened yet), *dare* to be that honest? But if I don't, I will have cheated again because that is how I really learnt, how we all learn, from our *mis*doing, even more than from our doings.

I already know that it's going to be a very good thing for me to do. Suddenly, too, I am beginning to understand what St. Paul meant when he said that it was in his weakness that he found his strength because then, as he put it, the power of Christ could find its way in. He was writing to the naughty and arrogant Corinthians, the yuppies of yesteryear, but the message is still true today. If you can't own up to your failings, you won't discover your strengths.

If the Americans really want to know about their potential leaders, they ought to ask each of them to take part in that radio series I'm doing, explaining what they have learnt in life, and how and when. Come to that, why shouldn't our own leaders do the same, be they in politics, business, public service, or, dare I say it, the Church? It might actually be a good way of celebrating the really important aspect of this week of hoo-ha: the fact that it is Adult Learners' Week, the time when we acknowledge that there are over forty million learners who aren't in school any more and who need urgently to discover their strength through their failings.

THE ANTIGONE
PRINCIPLE

I still remember the astonished looks on the faces of one lot of managers when they went into the classroom for the first session of their course. On each desk was a nice fat volume called *Understanding Company Accounts*. That was all right. They expected that. But on top of it was a much slimmer book—*Antigone* by Sophocles. "It's OK," I said. "It may be a Greek play, but it's in translation and it's your homework for tonight."

They wondered what kind of liberal arts course they had wandered into, but later that night they began to understand. Sophocles' play is about the dilemma of Antigone, whose brother has been killed by her uncle Creon in a battle for the control of Thebes. Creon had won and had issued an edict that her brother's body was not to be buried but was to lie outside the walls to be picked at by crows and vultures. Anyone who attempted to give him the rites of burial would die. Everything in Antigone screamed out that she must give the last rites to her brother. It was her overwhelming religious duty. Creon said, in his avuncular way, don't be silly; your first duty is to obey the law. Was it? Or was her first duty to do what was right even if it meant death? There was no comfortable answer; this was a Greek tragedy after all.

I did not need to remind those managers the next day that company accounts were not the most difficult problem they would face at work. More difficult at times is knowing when you should do far more than the company lays down, when you should overturn a rule or, in effect, break a bad law, the times, in other words, when principles and standards become more important than a quiet life.

Some people use Antigone's argument to justify disregarding laws or taxes which they feel unfair. Customs duties are fair game, it seems, and so was the poll tax when it was first introduced in Britain, but that is to belittle Antigone's dilemma. Don't make a moral principle out of an administrative duty, Jesus said once long ago, or, more grandiloquently, "Render unto Caesar the things that are Caesar's and to God the things that are God's." He had a point, I think.

Customs duties and poll taxes, however, are easy dilemmas, and so, in a way, was Antigone's life-or-death decision. It's the smaller, humdrum things that provide a bigger test. Should we at work, for instance, tolerate dirty, unhealthy, even dangerous conditions when we know that if we complain we'll be told to lump it or leave? Should we just stand by and let a colleague suffer the persistent nudge-nudge of sexual harassment, or should we make a stand?

Antigone knew that life would not be worth living if she was not true to her beliefs and her standards. My worry is that too often I, and I suspect a few others, are only too ready to settle for that life not worth living. Whenever I do, I know that I have diminished myself and, in a sense, denied my God.

THE WIN-WIN
CONTRACT

ℬ I am often reminded that the path to progress is not victory but compromise. For all to benefit, all must give. Compromise, however, sounds wrong—weak and indecent. Strong men, and strong women, stand firm; they brook no middle way for that is to admit defeat. That was the way that I, too, used to think. Convert them to my view, impose my will, dictate my terms; that way they would know who was boss. The trouble is that no one likes being bossed or dictated to, let alone defeated, so any deal I arranged could never be relied on; when the cat was away, the mice would undoubtedly play. The deals that work, I came to learn, are the deals where each party thinks that *they* won—"win-win contracts" they are sometimes called.

Obvious, perhaps, but the idea was a hard one for me to grasp. I had been brought up to fight my corner to the bitter end; success meant beating the opposition, which included even my own colleagues half of the time. It made for a world of envy, infighting, and suspicion. I lived life on a seesaw— jousting against my opposites, sometimes up and sometimes down; very energetic, but ultimately going nowhere, when it ought to have been at least a carriage going somewhere. You live and you learn. I sometimes say, half jokingly, that, like most men of my age, I am now on my second marriage, but it's to the same lady, which makes it much cheaper and more relaxing. What happened was that we used to have a seesaw marriage, but just when the seesaw was creaking badly, we turned the marriage into a win-win deal. Not competitors any more, in our various roles, but true partners with a renegotiated contract.

That turns out to be the key: we have to turn our competitors into partners if we want the deals to stick and the world to move, and you have to find a shared ambition for all those partners to justify their compromises. "Peace and Prosperity for All" will do very nicely at this time of year. We ought to have known all this a long time ago. Adam Smith wrote the *Wealth of Nations* in praise of the free market, but he had earlier written the *Theory of Moral Sentiments,* in which he said that a society's well-being depended on what he called "sympathy"—a fellow feeling for all those different from ourselves. We should not read one book without the other, for the Invisible Hand of the market needs an Invisible Handshake to make it work.

And, of course, long before Adam Smith, we were told to love our enemies. I used to think that both silly and impossible. Now I see that if we want to forge a lasting win-win contract, or to change a seesaw for a carriage going somewhere, then we have to learn to make our adversaries our allies.

BLINDED BY STEREOTYPES

℘ I was intending to say a few words this morning on summits and summitry, but I was diverted to more immediate matters by talking to the man who drove me back from the studio yesterday. He had been the export-sales director of a manufacturing firm, he told me, until two years ago, when the firm was taken over and closed down. After three months of unemployment and job hunting, he took up chauffeuring.

It has its compensations, he said—more time with the family, less worry, and he gets to meet some quite extraordinary passengers—but, at the age of forty-eight, with thirty years' experience, he feels that he could do more. But it's the thirty years' experience which counts *against* him, he finds, and the fact that he got his education in the university of life, with no degree to prove it. He is, to put it bluntly, too old even to get an interview.

He would have some sympathy, I felt, with those stern words in the Sermon on the Mount—"Strait is the gate, and narrow is the way which leadeth into it, and few there will be that will find it."

The preacher was talking about the path to salvation, but he could have been describing today's interview procedure. It goes like this, a friend who runs a computer-software company told me. "We need people with particular aptitudes for our work. Academic grades, age, or sex give no indication of those aptitudes. We do have a special test which does, but it costs a lot of money to administer. If, therefore, we need five new people, we are prepared to give the test to twenty. But there are three hundred applicants. How do we whittle these down to twenty? We choose the youngest with the best degrees. I know," he said, "that both these criteria are irrelevant. We could have chosen the tallest or all those with brown eyes, but we don't have that data on the forms, and it wouldn't be acceptable."

It can sometimes, then, be just administrative convenience not discrimination which closes the gate before we get to it, but that doesn't make it any easier to take. When we make our shortlists, we start with our stereotypes. Luckily those stereotypes don't matter so much when you are not buying chunks of people's lives but only their products or their services. I don't know the age of my plumber, and when I needed a piano tuner the other day, I did not specify age or sex. She turned out to be seventy and blind, which was actually an advantage in that calling.

I was intrigued by my son's first CV, compiled the other day. He is leaving drama school to enter the perilous world of the actor. I noticed that he had left out all references to his education. "But that's what got you where you are!" I expostulated. "I know," he said, "but the directors who audition me will only want to know what I did with it."

"Ye shall know them by their fruits," that sermon on the mountain went on. "You can't get grapes from thorns or figs from thistles." We should look at the fruits first, not the tree. If we do it the other way round, we risk blinding ourselves to the fruits of people's lives. If we changed our systems, we might change our stereotypes. "Judge not that ye be not judged," that sermon also said.

THE POINT
OF PRINCIPLE

ℬ N ot long ago I was sent another of those so-called personalized letters offering me the choice of a video-recorder, I think it was, cash, or a holiday for two if I went along to a sales pitch for a holiday time-sharing scheme. You've probably had one too—I think their mailing lists must be based on the telephone directory—and you probably threw it away. I'm afraid I'm a sucker, and on an earlier occasion I went along and was subjected to their high-pressure sales pitch. I managed to escape, I'm relieved to say, with my checkbook untouched *and* with my bribe; that time it was a miniature carriage clock.

Yes bribe—for that was what it was, and I had succumbed. The world seems increasingly full of bribes these days. Even the company-takeover game has turned into a bribery competition for shareholders, with not much obvious thought or attention paid to the people who work there or to the products they make. In effect every company in Britain and the United States is now potentially for sale to someone if the bribe is big enough and the bankers brave enough. You might even argue that the big share issues that went with the privatization of state industries in Britain were intended to bribe us all into the stock market, for good or ill.

It has to be distorting. Company boards now have to spend more time protecting their shares than managing their business, shareholders become traders not owners, we as individuals find ourselves pulled this way and that by enterprising seducers until we don't know which way is what. The world, for some people, seems overfull of choices.

I wouldn't want to do away with the choices. I feel far sorrier for the people with no choices at all than for those bewildered by them. So it is ultimately up to us.

"Choices are easier if you have principles," I found myself saying rather pompously to my son the other day. "What principles?" he said. "Yours?" "No," I said, ignoring the implied question, "*yours*, the only ones which actually stick are the ones you work out for yourself."

My son's dilemma was whether he should go on welfare, take the dole, while he was working full-time but for no money trying to build up his dance band and therefore not actually free for other work. "It's what everyone does," he said. "It's accepted practice. Having principles does not make the choice any easier."

Yes it does, but first you have to decide whether to follow your principles or "accepted practice." Why lose out, one feels, when everyone else is eating cake? That's the tough decision— principles or accepted practice? After that it's easy.

It would be nice, I think, if it once again became a compliment to say that someone was a man or woman of principle. It would stop our being slaves to accepted practice, would make many of our choices much easier, and would have saved me two hours of bombast and a miniature carriage clock.

THREE-FACED JUSTICE

ॐ "A fair day's pay for a fair day's work." That seems a sensible enough philosophy for a business to adopt. A just pay policy, you might say.

Unfortunately it isn't quite as simple as that, for justice has always been one of those good words that mean different things to different people, and so it is with the word *fair*. What seems fair to one can seem discrimination to another.

One view of justice, for instance, is that it means giving everyone what they need. That seems right and proper but so does the other definition: giving everyone what they deserve. Under the first definition those in need are the first priority, under the second those who work hardest and best come first. It's an issue which has split politicians between left and right down the ages. Give them what they need pulls to the left. Give them what they deserve pulls to the right. There's even a third definition of justice: giving everyone the same *unless* it is clear that giving someone a bit more benefits everyone—that is, giving special attention to the handicapped helps them to contribute to society, and, perhaps, giving great leaders big inducements benefits the rest of us.

What then is fair pay? Can it be right that one person be paid ten times more than another? "Yes," say some, "if he produces ten times as much." "No," say others, "because no one

126

needs ten times as much as another." "Yes," say others, "if that's what other people like him or her are getting." It's the old justice problem again.

I can see why it seems perfectly fair to some that the chairman of a company gets a $100,000 increase when the foreman gets $270. I can also see why it will seem grotesquely unfair to others. "Fair's fair" seems to beg an awful lot of questions. Nor can we leave it to the market. The market will tell us the going rate, which one might think would be the measure of what is deserved, one of the definitions of justice, but all markets are temporary and all are quirky or imperfect. It might be worth my while to pay the only plumber not on holiday in August an outrageous rate to mend my burst pipe, but that would not mean he deserves it. Markets, as they say, will tell you the price of anything and the value of nothing. Don't count on them for justice, that's for sure.

Justice, I think, wears different clothes in different circumstances. Robin Hood understood this—so does my entrepreneur friend who guarantees his employees a decent wage and a small share of the profits but takes for himself no wage but a large bonus when the good times come, trading security for risk. When you get it right, I think you know you've got it right. Only remember that there's always another definition, another side to the coin. Or, to put it more crisply, in the words of the prophet Micah, "Do justly, love mercy and walk humbly with your God."

THE MISSING
WORDS

Education in Britain in the end was something too important to be left to teachers. There is now a national curriculum enshrined in an Educational Reform Act (the new ERA they joke). Parliament has decided what our children should be taught.

It would no doubt disturb the splendid legal phraseology, but I would like to suggest that they insert somewhere in that Act three old-fashioned words—curiosity, forgiveness, and love—words which, to my mind, still lie at the heart of all learning.

I can tell you that they weren't much in evidence in my school, years ago. Curiosity there was called impertinence. If I learnt one lesson it was that all problems had already been defined and solved. The teacher knew the answer, so don't ask, memorize. Forgiveness? Why, to forgive was soft. So, if you erred, don't get caught. If you made a mistake, defend it to the death. Mistakes were punished not forgiven. And love, now that *was* a shocking thought. Grown men don't need anyone to care for them, praise them, or get excited by their successes. Nor should boys.

It didn't end with school. The first organizations I worked for didn't go in much for curiosity, forgiveness, and love either. Procedures, reprimands, and appraisal systems were, if I remember, their preferred devices.

128

Thank goodness, schools and organizations are different these days; they reflect a bit more the way we learn in life. In life, learning *has* to start with curiosity. If you don't ask questions, you won't get any answers from yourself or anyone else. Think of young children, poking their noses everywhere. Lose your curiosity and you become a cabbage.

Then come the mistakes. We all make mistakes when we try something new; look at young children again. But we won't learn from them unless we can accept that they are mistakes. Punish them and we get defensive; forgive them and we can work on them. Some organizations understand this now. I asked a personnel manager how he explained the success of his development program. "In one word," he said, "forgiveness. We give them big jobs. They make mistakes. We correct them, but we forgive them. They learn and grow."

And then there's love, or what my world calls "unconditional positive regard." Children will accept any rebuke from someone who they know loves them to distraction. Love the sinner, hate the sin. Grown men and women are no better; we can accept a rebuke much better if it comes from someone we know cares for us, come what may. We know too that warm encouragement brings out the best in us, as does support against the odds. Unconditional positive regard! Just call it love.

I wonder now about that biblical admonition that you can't get to heaven unless you become like little children. I wonder if perhaps Jesus isn't suggesting that the ways in which children learn should be our ways, our ways to reach our full potential, our full humanity. I wonder now why I never saw the Bible as a manual of learning theory. Curiosity, forgiveness, love—they are all there. It would be nice if they were also in the statute book!

ENTERPRISE
FOR WHAT?

℗ Britain's back in business, they say. More efficient now than West Germany at making steel, as good as the Japanese at making cars, even increasing her share of world trade again. Britain is no longer a businesspeople's joke, says *Fortune*, but a model of successful enterprise.

It's true. When I go to conferences of businesspeople abroad, they no longer smile behind their hands when the British talk. They lean forward now and listen respectfully. There's undoubtedly, too, a new self-confidence among Britain's business men and women and, yes, a new spirit of enterprise. It's true, and it has to be good that it is true because with more wealth we can do more things for more people, with more people.

But there has to be that "because." The wealth has to be there for a purpose. I met an Australian the other day who had come to England to escape what she saw as the crude commercialism of her own country. "But now that Britain is going the same way," she said, "I might as well be materialistic in the sun!"

The poet George Oppen once put it more dramatically. He wrote:

Wolves may hunt
With wolves, but we will lose
Humanity in the cities, stores and offices
In simple
Enterprise

(It could almost be a trailer for that film *Wall Street*.)

Enterprise, in other words, must not stop with enterprise or we lose our humanity. And if you believe that our humanity is of a special kind, that we are here to use our talents to make a difference to this world of ours, that we are meant to stand for something not just exist, then to lose your humanity is to lose your soul.

We cannot, however, duck out of the challenge because we fear the risks; we cannot forswear enterprise, success, and riches just because we might lose our way in them. No one ever said that riches were wrong, only that they made life more difficult. You have to be grown up to handle them; you have to have a purpose bigger than yourself if, that is, your life is ever going to be more than just a set of statistics.

The individuals whom I know who use their talents and their enterprise for purposes beyond themselves are those whom I most admire, whether they live richly or scantily. The same goes for companies. Those who are most exciting to work for are, often, the most profitable as well. Let us hope, and let us make sure, that the next *Fortune* article on Britain applauds not only our enterprise but its purpose.

IMAGE
ENHANCEMENT

I was sitting one day in a tiny, windowless room watching them edit a television documentary. "Wipe the traffic noise, Tim," the editor said. "Right," he said. "No—now it's a bit empty. What about some birdsong?" They went to the bookcase and took out a tape labeled "Birdsong." Suddenly the scene on the documentary came alive, with birdsong now, not traffic. "Hey, you can't do that," I exclaimed. "Why ever not?" They looked round at me, the naïve outsider. "Well," I said, "because it's not true; there weren't any birds there. It's a lie!" "Nonsense," they said, "it's just *image enhancement,* you wouldn't want us to film you with no clothes on, would you, so you dress up to look nice." Image enhancement, we're all at it all the time!

I suppose we are. I don't want the estate agent to tell prospective purchasers about the noise from the endless parties in the flat above, so I suggest that "convivial" might cover it if anyone asks. I even saw one house described as having central heating "sensibly confined to the ground floor"! I preen myself in front of the mirror to make sure that I look a touch slimmer and younger than I really am—just a little lie.

Most people would feel a bit of image enhancement does no one any harm. There are even courses on it if you feel the need. But at some stage image enhancement becomes a downright lie. How does one know where to draw that line? I don't know any general answer to that. What I do know, however, is that living a lie is very uncomfortable—unless of course your whole life is one big act, and I know a few people like that too! If we deceive *ourselves*, you might say, the truth is not in us. These words are actually a slight misquotation from St. John's Gospel. St. John really says, "If we say we have no sin, we deceive ourselves and the truth is not in us." In other words, no one expects people to be perfect; indeed we often like and respect people even more if we know their little frailties. Image enhancement can be counterproductive if it makes you, or it, seem too good to be true.

We should not, I think, be so afraid of ourselves. For many a year I tried to be something I wasn't with some fairly strenuous image enhancement. But the nice thing about growing older is that you eventually stop pretending. Then it is that you discover that being oneself, being truly oneself, is really rather fun. You can say what you like, see whom you like, tell it like it really is. What's more, it turns out that no one was taken in by the image anyway. These days I can vouch for it. "The truth will set you free."

JESUS WAS LAME

   A pril is the time for daffodils and for grass which grows too quickly. It is also, for some of us, the month for conferences.

Oh those conferences! Shut up in a hotel with a gaggle of people, most of them strangers, stooping to peer at each other's chests as we try to read our labels. And at every conference I seem to go through the same cycle. As soon as I arrive, depression deepens. Who are all those people? So imposing, so in command, intimidating almost. So glamorous, stars in their firmament. How can I compete? Yet most of them look depressingly boring, ugly even, at first sight. No way do I want to be marooned with these people.

Coward that I am, however, I don't escape. And always by the end the miracle has started to happen. The people now look different. That one who looked so imposing was after all just a shy soul hiding behind grim lips. The dumpy one in the ill-fitting suit was a bit of a genius with a lovely twist of humor. There are no ugly people now. Just individuals with different faces. Appearances are deceptive. Of course. But I think that there is more to it than that.

One of the nicest stories I've heard from the early Christian tradition has it that Jesus was lame. True or not I want to believe it. I would like to believe too that if He had lived a little bit longer He might also have been bald, like me. If Jesus was lame and maybe going bald, then no one mentioned it because no one noticed. Just imagine: those gospel writers writing about the most important man who ever lived and not one of them tells us what He looked like. So if Jesus was lame and no one noticed it, why? Because of what I believe Keats meant when he wrote, "Beauty is truth, truth beauty." Just that. Truth is beauty, beauty truth. The truth of who you are will always shine more strongly than what you look like.

Jesus was lame, and no one noticed. I find the idea very comforting as I stand in the bathroom in the morning, peering yet again at that drearily familiar face. Only be *true*, and no one will notice the body I inhabit.

Only be true—true to the best in oneself, true to one's beliefs, I suppose, true to what the Roman poet Lucretius called the essence of things. It's the secret of the meaning of life, I think, this truth—and of death come to that, when real truth comes to some for the first time. Only be true. But oh, how difficult it is—even at a conference with a label on my chest telling me who I am supposed to be.

HORIZONTAL
FAST TRACKS

⊘ Each year the BBC runs a competition in which listeners are asked to nominate and vote for the "Best of British Youth." There is always a shortlist of heroines and heroes who have defied life's odds to do good and notable deeds in their communities, often after failing their formal studies.

It all goes to strengthen my conviction that we are crazy to try to categorize people too soon, to fit them into predetermined slots. Character, happily, will keep breaking out.

The youngsters on the BBC list have, by their determination, found a niche where they can shine and can contribute. Even if *this* niche doesn't last forever, they will know *forever* that life has meaning. Too many of their generation must doubt that. Too many must see little point in life and no niches anywhere.

It was when I was in Japan to find out how they developed their young managers that they told me about their horizontal fast tracks. When the new recruits join the organization, they switch them from job to job in their first five years—the better they learn the faster they move—but horizontally, not upward as we do. "Why do you do this?" I asked. "It's obvious," they replied, which clearly it wasn't! It is not decreed that we should know our destiny or our talents at sixteen or even eighteen. All people should have different roles in different places with different people to find out what their special contribu-

136

tion can be, to make their first mistakes in safety, and to learn a nice variety of skills. "Is it not like that with you?" they said.

No. But it's a neat idea and not just for managers. Would it not be a better world if we could guarantee to *all* young people a protected horizontal track for three years or so after school or college, a time to find a slot that suited and a skill that pleased? They would need the proper training, of course, to fill each slot and help to find the confidence to move along the track. But we could do that, are already doing it in places.

It would be great for the economy, I bet, for we would once again have a workforce equal to the best. But it is not these utilitarian things that concern me most this morning. I see it as a moral duty, a charge on us, their elders, to give all young people the chance to find their niche in life and their talents as early as may be. It has to be a moral duty if you believe with me that there is for each one of us a God-given purpose in this world—for *each* of us, uniquely, and not just for the favored few.

Finding that purpose and that special niche is another matter. Few are granted the shaft of light that struck Paul on the Damascus road, and even he was well into his first career. God's purposes need human hands to take effect.

Let me put it this way: stealing people's futures is wrong, even if we do it by neglect.

HI-TOUCH
FOR HI-TECH

〒 This is a "Where were you when . . . ?" day! Where were you when, twenty-five years ago today, Neil Armstrong set foot on the moon— "One giant leap for mankind," as he famously said. I wonder how much of a leap it really was, looking back on it now, or whether it was the leap that we needed most.

I was thinking about that last weekend, over in Ireland, where my clan had gathered to celebrate the ninetieth birthday of my uncle. As a surprise, on the morning of his birthday, his two sons and their families had hired a helicopter. They landed it on the lawn outside his bedroom window and invited him to come for a trip, flying over his old Dublin haunts and back to his childhood home in the country. "It only took ten minutes," he said in some amazement. "When I was a boy, it took me three hours to cycle into Dublin. Later we got a car, and we could do it in just over an hour. Now it's ten minutes. What will it be like by the time I'm a hundred?" he wondered. Always intrigued by the future is my uncle, even now.

"That's the story of this century in a nutshell," I suggested to him. "We get to the same place, only quicker."

"The same place, yes, but the journey is different. You see so much more from the helicopter, but you feel less connected to it than you do on a bicycle."

Technology is indeed amazing, but it doesn't change the ultimate truth of things. It may even shield you from that truth. Another of those astronauts, Buzz Aldrin, has said that curing his drinking problem was much more difficult than flying *Apollo 11* to the moon. John F. Kennedy's vision of a race to that moon inspired the United States for a while, but gimmicks in space, no matter how sophisticated or bold, solve few of Earth's dilemmas. I still find it amazing that I can sit in a hotel room in Sydney, press a few buttons, and talk to my family in London, but that doesn't mean that we are a better family.

Like my uncle, I look to the future and its promise of ever more technological wonders with a greedy anticipation. The traveling will get quicker yet. Ironically, however, we shall have to work even harder to feel connected to the things that really matter. I was talking to another ninety-year-old recently, someone who had been born to great riches and great houses but had lost them long ago to war and revolution. She had lived in great poverty for most of her life, but it hasn't been at all bad, she said, because "I came to realize that 95 percent of the things that really matter are to do with people and their love, not with money or with things, and without the things you get closer to the people." Of course. But that's why more hi-tech needs ever more hi-touch to balance it. That, and the thought that we all get to the same place in the end, no matter how we travel.

PICTURE FRAMING

I once started a senior management course by asking the assembled managers what lay at the heart of their job. "Making decisions," they said. "Right," I replied. "Why don't you each come back here on Monday with your biggest decision of the week, and we'll discuss it." Next Monday the first manager said, rather shamefacedly, "Last week was rather odd, I didn't actually make anything that could be called a big decision." Neither it appeared had any of the others. "An odd week, then?" I asked. No, in fact a very normal week. The truth is that leaders don't only, or even mostly, make decisions in well-run systems.

What do they do then? Well, they spend a lot of time picking the people who pick the people who do make the decisions. I asked a school head once how he got the school to be the way he wanted it. "I pick the heads of departments and the heads of houses," he said, "and then I wait five years." But sometimes you don't have five years, and sometimes you find that your heads have already been picked for you or that you don't have an awful lot of choice. So what else do leaders do? What should the chairperson, the president, or the prime minister be worrying about? Reframing, I would suggest, not paintings but pictures in the mind. Good leaders are adept at reframing problems, at putting old facts into new bottles, at reconceptualizing the familiar so that new solutions leap up. Here's one example. A friend recently criticized an acquaintance of ours for bringing, as she put it, another bastard into the world. The word startled me. I hadn't heard it in its literal sense for ten years. Whoever coined the phrase *single-parent family* had reframed the whole situation so that new behaviors, new attitudes, and new laws became not only possible but obvious. There's an unsung leader there, somewhere. Do that for a whole nation or an organization and you set a sort of chemical reaction under way.

Mahatma Gandhi, to go to the other extreme, was a great reframer, turning a resistance movement from active to passive and so making it ultimately invincible. John Kennedy likewise— no great decision maker he, but his reframing energized a nation and part of the world. I wish we could train more people to be great reframers, but I fear that, even in the best of our business schools, we can only develop it a little if it's already there. Those who have it are blessed indeed and greatly needed.

This is the real challenge to all presidents, of countries or businesses, to do more creative reframing for their world, to create a picture of the task which gives meaning to existence and endeavor. But it is also a challenge for all those, in politics or management, in education or in the media, who aspire to lead others, for management is just a tug of war when the picture has no frame, and politics a petty squabble. I sometimes think that we forget that Jesus Himself took few decisions, gave few commands, did very little. If you wrote out His CV, it would read like the CV of a failure. We know now, of course, that He was reframing the picture—and changing the world. There's hope there for the rest of us; it is not our own dull CV that will be remembered but the pictures we reframed for others.

GYROSCOPES
FOR MORALS

ℬ꙰ Have you heard of the latest best-selling business book from the United States? It's called *The Ethics of Wall Street*, and it consists of 168 blank pages!

It is a sick joke. But it reminds me that the moral dilemmas of the financial world may be some sort of parable for the rest of us and indeed that part of our censorious attitude is fueled by the thought that "there but for the grace of God go I" or, to be rather more blunt, that "I wouldn't mind having a few of their dilemmas myself!"

Let's face it, it's a different world up there in London's financial center or in Wall Street. One has to remember, for instance, that the international money deals which the City makes add up, in the course of a year, to more than all the physical goods and services traded by this country. More than, did I say? Much more than. In fact, I'm told, thirty times more than.

But then money is used in two ways in that world. Some of it is ordinary money of the sort we all use to pay the wages and buy the groceries, but most of it is money as a commodity, money which people buy and sell, money money you might say. It must sometimes be very confusing to move from talking money money to ordinary money in the middle of a hectic day, and it's easy to understand how one might calculate a percentage in money money terms instead of in ordinary money. Nor would that matter too much if that money money didn't just occasionally end up as *real* money in a bank account or as a turbo-charged Porsche in the garage.

That's the problem, I think. One loses touch with what's real. It's like flying a plane in fog. You don't know whether you're upright or not unless there's a gyroscope in the cabin. Lose touch with reality and you lose your moral gyroscope and do things which in the cold light of day would *amaze* you. It happens in war, of course, but more ordinarily it can happen in any intense working atmosphere, in a hothouse advertising agency and in many a sales office. Shut out reality and you can lose your moral balance, do *anything* to get that sale.

Where do you look for the gyroscope then? Not to the people around you because they're in the same hothouse, like the eminent banker who, at the height of the City scandals, declared that insider dealing was a victimless crime. Not to laws, I feel, which deal only with extreme situations and usually after they have happened.

No, there *is* no gyroscope out there. We each have to look for it inside ourselves, and it's always there. I believe *that* because I believe that the spirit or essence of God is in each and every one of us whether we formally acknowledge it or not. Get in touch with that spirit and you are in touch with truth. As a city banker said to a bishop the other day, "Don't preach at us, help us to find spirituality." And it might be worth a Porsche to him to find his soul again.

MASACCIO'S
TRINITY

℘ I imagine that part of the thinking behind all these megabonuses to top executives is the assumption that they will motivate all us lesser mortals to aspire to the same sort of heights. No doubt that does work for those few panting at their heels, but most people, those whose salaries seem to lack a few zeros at the end, will probably get more depressed than motivated when they stop to think about it. "It really makes me wonder what life is all about," one young person said to me. "If these megabuck rewards are what society thinks are the real measure of a person's worth, then I might as well give up now. We're all going to die anyway, so why bother?"

I've had that feeling of ultimate futility myself, quite often in fact. On many a day, life seems to be just one long struggle toward the grave. Then one afternoon, I was lucky enough to go to the Church of Santa Maria Novella in Florence. There's a wonderful fresco there, by Masaccio, painted five hundred years ago when he was only about twenty-six. It's called the *Trinity* and is much admired for its mastery of perspective. But that was not what got me interested—and thinking.

The painting is of the crucifixion, with God the Father standing rather benevolently and protectively behind the cross, and the Holy Spirit, in the form of a dove, hovering between Him and the dead Christ. It was commissioned to decorate a merchant's tomb, and so, underneath the tableau, is a full-size painting of a stone tomb with a coffin inside—a see-through coffin, in fact, in which you can see the skeleton and, above it, an old Tuscan saying: "That which you are, I was. That which I am, you will be." A necessary reminder maybe, but depressing if it means that death is the only point of life.

Look up, however, to the scene of the crucifixion painted above. There is Christ hanging on the cross and, at its foot, Mary, his mother, and John, his best friend, looking up at him not in sadness, but in admiration and, almost, triumphantly. They seem to be saying, "What a great life that was!" To me that double painting says, "Yes, death is inevitable, but there is more to life than death, much more." That's the promise of the painting but also its challenge because the "more" is going to be different for each one of us, and it is up to us, and only us, to discover what it is before we die. And how will it be measured if and when we find it? Not, I think, in money but by the look in the faces of our friends and of all those whom our life has touched when they finally contemplate our death.

DEGREES FOR LIFE

ast week was the week of congregations. I don't mean church congregations, but the degree ceremonies which universities call congregations, those occasions when they assemble their new graduates and the proud parents in sports halls, marquees, and even cathedrals to present them with their credentials.

They are "good news" days, these congregations, bright moments in gloomy times, but the best bits for me, as one of the onlookers, are the honorary degrees. Dressed up in brightly colored robes and medieval scholars' caps, these distinguished citizens get to hear their lives extolled by an orator before doffing hats and shaking hands with the chancellor of the university. It is a sort of obituary for the living, your life spread out before you in public with all the warts decently concealed.

All sorts of people get them. At one congregation which I attended last week, there were two distinguished scientists, a novelist, a bus driver turned Methodist preacher, the arts editor of the local paper, and a lady who had devoted most of her life to building up a literary society in the region. They were being honored for their very different contributions to life and society.

John Gielgud put it rather well, I thought, in the last of the Inspector Morse films. He was playing the role of Chancellor of the University and was obviously reveling in it. At the luncheon before the degree ceremony he addressed one unfortunate U.S. academic as "Mr." "It's really Dr.," protested the American. "I got my Ph.D. in chemistry." "Indeed," snorted Gielgud. "All *my* degrees are honorary ones. You only had to pass an examination to get yours. I had to earn mine by my life!"

You can earn your degrees by your life, as you do the citations which go with them, those obituaries for the living. I sometimes ask my management students, as an exercise, to compose their own obituaries in advance. That sounds bizarre because they are only in their mid-thirties, but I ask them to suppose that they live to a ripe old age and that their best friend is to read their eulogy at their memorial service, so write it for him or her.

Writing your own obituary forces you to work out how you want to be remembered and for what. It is equivalent to awarding yourself an honorary degree in life. It is an opportunity which we all have, at any age, to make sense of our lives, to redeem them—that is, to compensate for any failings or inadequacies along the way. When St. Paul said that Jesus redeemed us all by his death, he didn't mean that we had, therefore, no responsibility for our own lives. The Prayer Book has it right when it has us offer thanks for the *means* of grace and the *hope* of glory. It is still up to us, with that help, to earn our own honorary degrees.

Would it not be great, I thought, if the churches had the job of awarding those degrees. That would really fill our cathedrals with congregations.

THE COMPOST
THEORY

   I recently heard the voice of the Bishop of Durham coming over the airwaves. He was saying, as always, interesting and provocative things about eternal damnation, only to be at once corrected by another bishop. The dear old Church of England is at it again, I thought, airing its squabbles in public. No, I reminded myself, it's only the compost heating up.

It was a friend, a clerical friend, who first introduced me to the compost theory of the Church. Compost in a heap is a smelly mess. Spread it around, however, and it does a power of good. It's the same with the Church. Members of the Church come together to renew themselves and fortify themselves by prayer, worship, and debate, then go forth for their work of mission in the world—God's compost, you might say.

The trouble is that, on the whole, most of us come across the Church only when it is in the compost heap, when it is not always an enviable sight or smell. We don't always notice it when it is hard at work in the soil. But if the compost theory really worked, then the two million or so who are regular churchgoers would probably be enough to invigorate a nation, provided, of course, they were properly composted and properly spread around. Sadly, a lot of the compost never leaves the heap and doesn't want to. Sadly, too, a lot of the compost heaps don't work too well. I can't say that the average parish service really

148

charges me up and sends me out into the world, as the Prayer Book says it should, "to live and work to the glory of God."

Luckily, however, there are other and unsuspected ways to fuel our energies for good. This year, too late in life I fear, I got to know and love the paintings of Piero della Francesca and followed his trail to San Sepulcro, the small town in Umbria where he lived half a millennium ago. There I saw his fresco of the Resurrection, painted onto the wall of what is now the Civic Museum. It is a famous painting, but seeing it for real is quite a shock. Christ is painted rising out of the tomb, a Christ with a surprisingly modern face and modern haircut—a Christ for our times, I felt.

Sleeping soldiers are propped against the side of the tomb, unaware of what is happening. It is the eyes of the Christ figure that haunt you. They look at you and into you. They said to me, "Now is your chance to be resurrected, to redeem your life, to be a new you, a true you, and to leave your sleeping past behind. And you can be sure," said the eyes, "that you will be able to do it because if I can, You can." It haunts me, that fresco; it challenges me and inspires me. Who would have thought that I would have found my compost heap in the Civic Museum in San Sepulcro?

SPG

ॐ Every year, it seems, the big banks decide to write off tens and hundreds of millions of pounds, dollars, yen as provision against bad debtors; sometimes it is because some Third World countries have not repaid their loans but sometimes, recently, it has been because some big businesses which they helped to finance have regrettably collapsed. Just occasionally I wonder why it is that when the banks do this they are commended for their prudence, but if ever I, in my small way, were to make such gross errors of judgment it would be called an unforgivable mistake. It's wonderful what you can do with words.

Words and money mattered too in the Irish rectory where I grew up. Each week my parents would prepare and exchange their personal accounts, in an attempt to keep some track of their spending. It was a weekly agony for my mother, who could never remember what she had spent on what. I used to try to help. "Why," I once asked, "do you spend so much sometimes on the SPG when we are so poor?" A child of the rectory, I knew about the SPG; it was the Society for the Propagation of the Gospel in Foreign Parts, a famous missionary society. "Hush," said my mother, "and never tell your father, but SPG really stands for Something, Probably Grub."

It was my first realization that accountancy can sometimes be more of a creative art than a science. Looking back now I think that my father always knew and she knew that he knew, but they both realized that "keeping count" was a valuable discipline, even allowing for the SPG.

Digging deeper, I came to realize that it is part of the tradition of every religion that we should have to render an account of our life at the end of that life. It would be prudent, therefore, that we should prepare for ourselves, from time to time, some interim accounts, some trial balances, showing what we have taken from life so far and what we have put back into it.

Balance sheets should balance. There should be as much on the giving side as on the getting side; and balance sheets should grow. Empty and emptying people haven't much to give. Of course, I am not talking money now. Other things are rather more important when it comes to measuring one's *spiritual* net worth. To each of us, there are some special assets given, to be used not wasted. Perhaps it is time for an audit.

The difference is that if, by laziness or error, our spiritual net worth declines in one accounting period, then, lucky us, we are not written off, there is no heavenly receivership, just the expectation that things will be noticeably better in the period ahead. I am forgiven but not released. That's tough spiritual banking, but, I think, good banking.

POSTSCRIPT
THE MYSTERY
OF THE UNIVERSE

 I am no poet, but I was once asked to try my hand at poetry, to provide some of the words for a musical cantata. Here it is—the beginnings of a philosophy of religion.

There is a mystery at the heart of things.

Why don't we die?
So much of life is worry, toil and tears
Why do we strive so busily to stay alive?
Why not just die?

What is Beauty made of?
We love the beauty in a sunset, a painting or a face
We know it's beauty when we see it, but who can say
What makes it so?

And then there's Joy
How good it is to laugh, to sing, to dance
To see the eyes of children smile—but who
Invented Joy?

There is this mystery at the heart of things

Or what of Love?
Why should we care for others, or put another first?
Why need the love of others to be whole ourselves?
A strange thing Love.

Whence comes our Energy?
So many strive each day to build a better world,
Putting heart and body to a stringent daily test,
Why do they bother?

What keeps us Good?
When the way ahead is snared with tempting traps
Like sloth and gluttony, or selfishness and greed.
Whence comes our virtue?

There is more mystery at the heart of things

Could it be chance?
We all are just a random mix of genes
Our feelings chemistry, our bodies particles in flight.
Is it all luck?

Or is there something?
Some force or reason, some point behind it all
Something that hounds us on, for each to find
A Spirit and a Truth?

Is there a mystery in the heart of things?

Note

The cantata "The Mystery of the Universe" with music by Barrie Guard, played by Andy McCullough and the Clarinet Connection, with the words narrated by Judi Dench, was published as a record by ICY Records, P.O. Box 94, SW1W 9EE, in 1987.